The Pleasures
of Leisure

Also by Robert Dessaix

Fiction
Night Letters: A Journey through Switzerland and Italy
Corfu

Non-fiction
A Mother's Disgrace
Secrets with Drusilla Modjeska and Amanda Lohrey
(and so forth)
Twilight of Love: Travels with Turgenev
Arabesques: A Tale of Double Lives
On Humbug
As I Was Saying: A Collection of Musings
What Days Are For

Edited
Picador New Writing
Australian Gay and Lesbian Writing: An Anthology
*Speaking Their Minds: Intellectuals and the Public
Culture in Australia*
The Best Australian Essays 2004
The Best Australian Essays 2005

The Pleasures of Leisure

Robert Dessaix

KNOPF

A Knopf book
Published by Penguin Random House Australia Pty Ltd
Level 3, 100 Pacific Highway, North Sydney NSW 2060
www.penguin.com.au

Penguin
Random House
Australia

First published by Knopf in 2017

Addresses for the Penguin Random House group of companies can be
found at global.penguinrandomhouse.com/offices.

National Library of Australia
Cataloguing-in-Publication entry

Dessaix, Robert, 1944- author
The pleasures of leisure / Robert Dessaix
9780143780045 (hardback)

Leisure – 21st century – Anecdotes
Recreation – 21st century – Anecdotes
Work-life balance – Anecdotes

Cover illustrations courtesy of Shutterstock
Cover design by Nada Backovic
Internal design by Midland Typesetters, Australia
Typeset in 12/16 pt Adobe Garamond by Midland Typesetters, Australia
Printed in Australia by Griffin Press, an accredited ISO AS/NZS
14001:2004 Environmental Management System printer

Penguin Random House Australia uses papers that are natural, renewable
and recyclable products and made from wood grown in sustainable
forests. The logging and manufacturing processes are expected to conform
to the environmental regulations of the country of origin.

Contents

Preamble

How do we learn to occupy the great rooms
of the hours that open before us
each morning? It's as though time itself
enters with the light, the first birdsong,
saying THERE – find something to cover this
empty floor, get yourself by some means across
to the other side.

Lauris Edmond, 'Going North', in *A Matter of Timing* (1996)

There is disquiet spreading rapidly across the globe about empty time. It's hardly new: both the Greeks and the Romans were apt to get edgy about it, punishing laziness with death; even easeful living struck many Romans of the late republic as a kind of dereliction of duty. All of a sudden, though, there's a note of panic creeping into our consternation.

For a start, why is there so little empty time? We were supposed to be awash in it by now – technology and progressive politics have been promising us freedom from toil for over a century – yet, astonishingly, there's less of it about than in our grandparents' day. (Except in Italy, as you'd expect.) Paradoxically, the richer we get, the harder we work and the less time we have to do what we want. What's gone wrong?

Furthermore, what do we want? When we actually find ourselves with a couple of hours or a week or even the rest of our lives to spend precisely as we please, most of us don't know what to do with the unoccupied time. Should we log in to Facebook? Watch the Tigers play the Roosters? Keep bees? Fix the fence? Learn Greek? Stay in bed? Nobody – or at least nobody we might look up to – seems to be sure. Once upon a time we had Bertrand Russell and John Maynard Keynes offering us advice on the subject, not to mention Jesus and Theodor Adorno, but nowadays there's nobody – or nobody with much authority. Alarm is growing apace.

Certain entrepreneurs are busy finding ways to turn this anxiety into money by medicalising it, by selling us yet more technology, or packaging the emptiness up as tennis lessons, say, or trekking or a massage, and selling it back to us at a profit – most agreeably in many cases. However, when the mass of humanity in economically developed societies does find itself with a free moment or two, it frequently chooses to sit slumped in front of the television or fiddles with a mobile device. The nobility, needless to say, have never been at a loss for something enlivening to do while others toil on their behalf – they gamble, collect art, shoot wild animals, hold charity balls and so on – but their ranks are thinning fast. (The rich, we must remind ourselves, are not the nobility – by and large they're not even the gentry.)

In brief, it's high time we faced these two critical questions head-on: why, despite all the advances in science and compound interest, in Keynes' pithy formulation, is there so little free time in our lives (except in Italy) and why, when vacant time does open up for us, are we so clueless about what to do with it? At the heart of both our inability to jump off the treadmill of toil and our bewilderment about what to do next if we do, lies confusion, I believe, about the meaning of leisure. Does leisure largely mean entertainment? Idleness? Playing sport? Taking up a hobby? Few of us have given it much concentrated thought.

I hadn't really given the matter much thought myself until, in middle age, I read *The Talented Mr Ripley*. Early on in Patricia Highsmith's novel, Tom Ripley, a sexually ambiguous, amoral con artist from Boston, Massachusetts, becomes a man of leisure (Highsmith's word, not mine) simply by beating young Dickie Greenleaf to death with an oar in a picturesque Italian setting and then embezzling the lavish inheritance. They were quite fond of each other at first, but when Dickie began to tire of Ripley, the relationship soured. After a spate of adventures in exotic locales and two more murders, Ripley goes on in subsequent novels to live a life of elegant ease in a villa near Fontainebleau with a beautiful, wealthy wife of whom he also seems fond, if less so than he once was of Dickie, dabbling when moved to do so in a little murder and fraud, just to keep his hand in.

For people like Tom Ripley – and, indeed, like Dickie Greenleaf before him – leisure comes naturally. They effortlessly 'occupy the great rooms / of the hours that open before [them] / each morning' without toil or conscience. Both indulge in a little activity for profit from time to time, but mostly they choose to live for pleasure. They live 'lightly and gayly', to quote the celebrated Chinese thinker and champion of idleness Lin Yutang. Both Russell's and Keynes' younger contemporary, Lin liked to call himself a 'loller' in English, despite starting and ending his life as a Presbyterian.

'Scamps' was another of Lin's favourite words and scamps are exactly what Tom and Dickie are: they both arrive more or less nonchalantly at a 'keen and intense joy of living'. They have a lot more fun than I ever did, yet are far less virtuous.

On reading Highsmith's novel twenty-odd years ago I realised with a start that leisure was something I'd never quite got the hang of. I still regret this, although not bitterly. I was certainly never idle: I knew how to fill vacant time usefully and productively, and did. You couldn't have called me a scamp, either, not even on school excursions, and I'd never nonchalantly arrived at anything at all (although from an early age, by dint of hard work, I could say 'nonchalant' in several languages). On the contrary, all my life I'd cared deeply about ideas, skills and causes, playing no games unless forced to, not even Snap, and certainly not cricket. Playing, as I understood it, was something you did on the piano in as accomplished a fashion as possible. I had no hobbies – like the humourless Adorno, I'd have been horrified that anyone might consider my pastimes 'hobbies', 'mindless' preoccupations aimed purely at killing time – and I would be hard-pressed to name any hobbies I have now, despite no longer having any objection to hobbies. Is perusing atlases for fun a 'hobby'? It's about all I've got. I was not a popular boy at school – or anywhere else, for that matter. I was a Calvinist, broadly speaking, forever striving to prove by my industry and its fruits that I was one of God's elect. Like most Calvinists, since I was not idle I could see no good reason why anyone else should be. I blame my mother for this resistance of mine to any idea of leisure – to any notion of self-abandonment, really: like Lin Yutang she began and ended her life a Presbyterian, but as a late adoption I only knew her towards the end. For all that, I must emphasise that I was far from joyless: I was a busy little bee. Still, I could have done with less caution. A line from one of Rimbaud's poems – strictly speaking a knightly lament – comes to mind in this regard: '*Par délicatesse / J'ai perdu ma vie.*' ('Through lack of boldness I've wasted my whole life.') In reality there was nothing meek or dainty about Arthur Rimbaud, and he hadn't wasted his life by any stretch of the imagination, but the line strikes a chord with me.

Reflecting on leisure, finally, has brought me alive in ways I could never have foreseen. Why there's less and less time for it in advanced economies is fairly clear, I think. There are two principal culprits. Bertrand Russell put his not particularly left-wing finger on the first of them nearly a century ago in his celebrated essay 'In Praise of Idleness': leisure needs to be shared around. However, the modern capitalist system favours overwork for some and unemployment for others, making everyone miserable to produce what everyone could be happier producing if they all worked less. For its part, socialism in the twentieth century eliminated unemployment through a system of total work: everyone except the priestly class (the Party) worked full-time all the time at half-speed, enjoying a limited range of State-approved leisure activities during limited time off. As a result, the masses lived if not wretched then broken-spirited lives, punctuated with outbursts of abandonment. That, at least, is how it worked in Eastern Europe during my time there as a young man. Left-wingers for the most part take themselves so seriously, I find, even when cogitating on leisure: so much false consciousness to correct, so little time to do it in. Even Bertrand Russell can be a bit po-faced about fun. Perhaps in Cuba it's different.

The second culprit is quite simply greed. What both of the dominant political systems in league with the industrial revolution have produced is an inordinate lust for more – more possessions, bigger houses, more cars, newer technology, more *things*. We are insatiably addicted to things, and have been since at least the Great Exhibition of 1851, trading free time for the chance to accumulate more of them – and not one of the great philosophers foresaw this. So we work until we drop. Things can give pleasure, of course (I love my Clarice Cliff vase, my Indonesian ikats, my handmade messmate table), but we've gone overboard: as Jerome K. Jerome put it more than a century ago, 'We have turned the world into a workshop to provide ourselves with toys.' In other words, to purchase luxury we have sold our ease. Never mind about toys: do not even sell yourself 'for the means of life', Keynes admonished us in his 'Economic Possibilities for our Grandchildren', but strive to 'keep alive, and cultivate into a fuller perfection, the art of life itself'. I doubt many of us these days would even know what he was talking about.

We row frantically like galley slaves towards retirement and then, having arrived, and freed from the lash, we find that instead of all the time in the world, we're staring into infinite nothingness. 'This arrest of habit,' Janet Frame once cruelly wrote, 'often coincides with a permanent arrest of the heart.'

How obtusely proud we are these days of being busy! Yet to be busy is actually to advertise one's own enslavement. 'There is nothing the busy man is less busied with than living,' Seneca wrote two thousand years ago. Seneca had little sympathy for those who claimed to be busy for the sake of their children, either, or future generations: he called this being 'wasted for the sake of another'. Who would then be wasted for the sake of yet another. And so on, ad infinitum. Robert Louis Stevenson considered 'extreme busyness, whether at school or college, kirk or market' to be a 'symptom of deficient vitality'.

For any of this commitment to working, as opposed to living freely, to make sense to us, we have to have some notion of Paradise in the offing: an afterlife, for example, the future socialist paradise on earth, or at the very least a period of taking our ease for a few years before we die. In the absence of a future paradise, work looks much less appealing. As Donald Barthelme said, 'The death of God left the angels in a strange position.'

Work, however agreeable, useful or necessary, is essentially a form of servitude. The aim of leisure is first and foremost to make us masters of our own time, as one never is when working. But what is it?

To begin with I was in two minds about one of leisure's key components: idleness. Is it a virtue or is it a vice? In Dickie Greenleaf's case, for instance, it's portrayed as a vice: the man does nothing but spend his allowance on loose living in Italy. In Tom Ripley's, however, there's a virtuosity to his idleness, a focused exploitation of his talents, which we might well admire, even if we do not approve of his morals. Tom Ripley is never lazy. In other words, while there's little mystery (or so it would seem) about the nature of most other leisure activities such as games, hobbies and the myriad forms of entertainment available for us to enjoy nowadays, idleness remains ambiguous.

Throughout history the privileged classes have tended to disapprove of idleness amongst those propping up their privileges. For them idleness has meant sloth. The emperors Theodosius II and Justinian, for instance, had stringent dob-in-an-idler laws allowing Byzantines of a certain class to make slaves out of those they denounced to the authorities. A thousand years later Henry VIII, with an eye to encouraging industry in his kingdom, declared that idleness, as opposed to his own leisure pursuits, caused Almighty God 'high displeasure' and brought ruin, decay and impoverishment to the realm. The penalties could include mutilation and hanging. His successor, Edward VI, was hardly more indulgent, making it clear in his Injunctions of 1547 that, as he saw it, idleness led inevitably to drunkenness, brawling, begging, stealing and even murder. To prevent this fall into riot and moral turpitude, he recommended an occupation and a craft. Again, he was no doubt thinking less of the idle amongst his own entourage, with their diverse sports and entertainments, than he was of the slothful amongst the labouring classes. He too feared that idleness would lead to the impoverishment of the realm. Or at least his advisors did: Edward was only ten years old when his Injunctions were made public.

By way of contrast, for just as many millennia some thinkers and writers have called 'idleness' in one form or another the highest form of life. For them, all work, even the most pleasurable and useful, is slavery by another name. Leisure, on the other hand, is freedom. Some have understood idleness to mean doing as little as possible, rather like the lilies of the field that neither toil nor spin, Solomon in all his glory still failing to be arrayed like one of them. Someone had to toil and spin to produce Solomon's raiments for him, even if not Solomon himself, but in the case of the lily nobody toiled at all. This arrangement is difficult to replicate at this point in history.

In feudal Japan the Buddhist poet Kenkō, in his *Essays in Idleness*, asked how anyone 'who feels the vanity of the world' and wishes to pass beyond the confines of life and death could 'devote himself day and night to the service of his lord'. It is better altogether, he wrote, and more seemly, to give up all tasks and be at leisure. Not that Kenkō was in favour of laziness or disapproved of seeking a sense of accomplishment in what we do, but he warned against spending our lives in servitude to a master – or to our lust for possessions or to our appetites. Foremost in his thought as a Buddhist monk was his awareness of the folly of yoking ourselves to impermanence.

In the late 1750s, with the first whiff of the industrial revolution in the air, Samuel Johnson began publishing a series of essays under the byline 'Idler' in the *Universal Chronicle*, claiming that everyone 'is, or hopes to be, an Idler'. By idleness Johnson appears to have meant something not unlike what I mean by indolence: staying

in bed until noon and doing as little as possible for the
rest of the day, while remaining, it must be pointed
out, fiercely curious. This idea of doing nothing, or
at least nothing of any consequence most of the time,
seems to have appealed to a multitude of other thinkers
and writers (of a certain class) both before and since:
Aristotle, Tacitus, Seneca and Michel de Montaigne
(whose mind famously became a 'runaway horse' when
he was idle); Jean-Jacques Rousseau, whose great delight
was to 'fritter away the whole day inconsequentially
and incoherently, following the whim of the moment';
and more recently (and amusingly) Jerome K. Jerome,
who co-edited a magazine called *The Idler* from 1892 to
1911 and confessed that idling (not to be confused with
sheer slothfulness) 'always has been my strong point'
and kept his 'boat of life' light; Anton Chekhov, whose
'most intense pleasure' it was to 'sit doing nothing . . .
[or] doing useless things'; and modern British idling
wits such as G. K. Chesterton, who believed that doing
nothing was the purest and holiest thing anyone could
do; the anarchist S. L. Lowndes, who maintained that
only fools work voluntarily, the rest being either bribed
(in the case of single people) or blackmailed (in the
case of the married) into doing it; the mischievous
Tom Hodgkinson (author of *How to Be Idle* and *The
Idle Parent*); Stephen Robins (*The Importance of Being
Idle*); and Milan Kundera, according to whom sitting

on a hillside with a dog doing nothing was 'to be back in Eden'.

Yes, that's right – they're all men. And all of them have nothing but contempt for busy bees. It's hard to say who they thought would work the fields and slaughter the animals for their tables, build the roads, spin their cloth, erect and heat their houses, cook their food and print the publications they wrote for: those whose job it was to do so, presumably. As Lin Yutang put it, fore-shadowing Lowndes, there will always be fools aplenty ready and eager to make themselves useful while the wise bask in life's simpler, and idler, joys. I'm not sure this quite covers the matter: it's all too easy to dismiss those forced to labour to stay alive as 'fools'.

With this in mind, another group of writers and thinkers take a more active, more alert view of what idleness ideally is. Here we might think of Russell in particular, who loathed the idleness (or indolence, perhaps) of those who lived off the labour of others, while promoting an increase in leisure as a goal for everybody. Without leisure, Russell believed, mankind would never have emerged from barbarism, but what exactly leisure comprises, Russell didn't say.

For many other thinkers, too, idleness is best under-stood not so much as the freedom to do nothing but the freedom to do anything. In this case it is redolent of 'doing nothing to some purpose', to quote Alan Bennett.

time you enjoy wasting is not wasted time

In fact, it starts to take on aspects of what many nowadays call 'mindfulness': a kind of vigorous, centred inactivity.

Robert Louis Stevenson, author of 'An Apology for Idlers' (1877) as well as his more celebrated fictions, is one of the most quoted writers on the subject of idleness. For Stevenson, freeing yourself from work requires a level of imagination – a generous nature, in his terms – distressingly few can muster. (It also requires an income, but Stevenson's focus lies elsewhere.) A faculty for idleness, he said with great insight, implies a strong sense of who you are. Indeed, good leisure, as we shall see, which partakes of idleness, is the very enactment of who you have most strongly felt yourself to be. To put it another way, through leisure we rediscover both our raw nature and our cooked one – both who we are and the roots of our own civilisation. It does not consist of doing nothing, but, on the contrary, 'doing a great deal not recognised in the dogmatic formularies of the ruling class' – indeed, for Stevenson, idleness, properly understood, is an industry in itself.

As I began to think more and more deeply about leisure and both its pitfalls and possibilities, I began to look about me more attentively to see who seemed to be occupying the vacant rooms that opened up each morning in an enlivening, pleasurable way, covering the empty floor and getting 'across / to the other side', as Lauris Edmond put it in her poem, with more than just work and pruning the roses – and more than just mucking about in boats, with the odd dalliance and riff on the saxophone thrown in, like Dickie Greenleaf. Was there anyone? At this point in history there is little that can be done immediately about the materialism fuelling the general addiction to work, but new ways of thinking about magnifying the time that's our own should be possible, as should good ways for us to fill it. I began to think about dogs and fecundity.

The thing about pack animals such as dogs and humans is that, once they've eaten what they killed or rooted about and gathered, or, in the case of humans and domestic animals, somebody else killed or rooted about and gathered, they lie down and have a nice snooze. Some species snooze for days, others lounge about, dropping off from time to time – in a word, loafing. Then they commonly engage in a spot of nesting and grooming with their companions – patrolling the boundaries, seeing to the bedding, combing out vermin, indulging in a bout or two of foreplay and copulation with a partner or good friend. And then they play, both competitively and for the fun of it, in many cases resorting to a parodic, playful version of the activities that came before the snooze (play fighting, play hunting, play feasting, play communing ecstatically with higher realities and so on), but sometimes just frolicking. Everything they do – we do, you do, I do – after the meal is leisure. It's *otium* in Latin, rather than its opposite, *negotium*. Humans tend to cram all the hunting and gathering (the *negotium*) into the middle part of their lives, leaving pitifully few years at the end for loafing, nesting and fun – for *otium*; dogs tend to do no work at all, snooze endlessly and play in short bursts. This book is a clarion call for balance.

Leisure, as I see it now, is the word we use in English to cover a wide range of loafing, nesting, grooming and play activities, freely chosen purely for the pleasure they afford us, never for material gain, even if they also turn out to be of practical benefit to us and to others. Virtuosity is more important than virtue when we're at leisure. Leisure, wisely chosen, makes even the shortest life deep. At leisure, it transpires, we are at our most intensely and pleasurably human.

Robert Dessaix
Hobart, Tasmania

Loafing

I loafe and invite my soul,
I lean and loafe at my ease observing a spear of summer grass.

Walt Whitman, 'Song of Myself' (1855)

. . . the most precious, the most consoling, the most pure and
holy, the noble habit of doing nothing at all – that is being
neglected in a degree which seems to me to threaten the
degeneration of the whole race.

G. K. Chesterton, 'A View of William the Conqueror' (1927)

Doing nothing

'There's really no point in doing anything in life,' Monsieur Gustave, the concierge, observes acidly in *The Grand Budapest Hotel*, 'because it's all over in the blink of an eye . . . and the next thing you know, rigor mortis sets in.' By your early fifties – Ralph Fiennes' age when he played Monsieur Gustave – this is something that may well have occurred to you. But is it true? The day I saw the movie the audience tittered nervously – but it *was* Good Friday, so we were all a bit uneasy anyway.

At this point in the movie Monsieur Gustave is sitting with his Lobby Boy, Zero, in a First Class train compartment over a glass of Pouilly-Jouvet '26 ('so we don't have to drink the cat-piss they serve in the dining car'). It's the perfect setting (and Fiennes is brilliant in the role): in less opulent surrounds, world-weariness can sound like whingeing. His snappish remark is particularly apropos because he and his Lobby Boy are actually dashing to view the rapidly stiffening body of the Dowager Countess Céline Villeneuve Desgoffe und Taxis, one of the many well-born ageing blondes amongst guests from across the continent to whom he has provided 'exceptional services'. 'As the years go by,' he explains to the inscrutable Zero, 'you have to move on to the cheaper cuts.' He hopes, he says, to have been left a few klubecks in the Countess's will.

As I sit here, well past fifty, marooned in the lobby of my own grand hotel, the Mayfair, Darjeeling, staring out at the fog, Monsieur Gustave's words are fresh in my mind. I have been doing more or less nothing for several days. The Mayfair is not quite the Grand Budapest, despite once having been the summer retreat of the zamindar of Nazargunj, but it's perched, like the Grand Budapest, on the edge of a ridge above a valley so deep I've never managed to see the bottom of it. Alas, unlike the Grand Budapest's guests, we have no funicular to take us there. In fact, because of the fog I haven't seen much at all since leaving Calcutta. A few cows and cyclists down on the plain around the airport, but up here in Darjeeling and last week on the tea estate across the valley just billowing greyness.

To be honest, I've done virtually nothing for the last week or two. I've brought two or three books with me to read – a slim Anita Brookner, *The Rules of Engagement*, which is growing on me (I think), and Goncharov's *Oblomov* ('a monument to human idleness', it says on the cover), which I'm about halfway through – but I haven't much been in the mood for either. Have I ever read *Oblomov* or do I just think I must have? Tolstoy declared himself 'in raptures' over it and Chekhov marvelled at Goncharov's talent. It's a masterpiece, no doubt about it, but I'm hankering after something a touch spicier.

The thing to catch sight of up here if you can is Kanchenjunga, the third highest mountain in the world – it's all anyone talks about, really. On the tea estate everyone leapt out of bed at six every morning to peer north into Nepal, hoping for a glimpse of it. Once or twice there was a whitish smudge in the grey, but mostly they just saw fog. Here at the Mayfair the Indian family I meet at breakfast has got up in the dark at 4.30 every morning to rush to Tiger Hill to see the first rays of the sun set fire to the Himalayan peak. They, too, have seen nothing. They are visibly dispirited.

So here I am this afternoon, befogged again, again doing pretty much nothing. Not quite, but almost. Monsieur Gustave may have hit the nail on the head when he said there was no point in doing anything in life, but doing nothing at all on any given afternoon is not as easy as it sounds. Even if you think that, at a certain point in the day – indeed, at a certain point in life itself – with the hunting and gathering done and the fruits of it consumed, it's natural to do nothing, in practice in Western society what could 'doing nothing' actually mean?

When you ask a teenager what he's doing, for example, and he says 'Nothing,' he doesn't really mean nothing, he means 'Leave me alone.' Christopher Robin likes doing 'Nothing' best of all, or so he tells Pooh Bear, but when Pooh asks him how you do Nothing,

Christopher Robin is less than clear: 'Well, it's when people call out at you just as you're going off to do it, What are you going to do, Christopher Robin, and you say, Oh nothing, and then you go and do it.' 'Oh, I see,' says Pooh, who doesn't see at all.

Monsieur Gustave himself, as a member of the serving classes, is almost frenetically busy throughout *The Grand Budapest Hotel.* We never see him doing nothing. And hardly have he and Zero arrived at the Dowager Countess's family castle to view the corpse when mayhem erupts: he absconds with a painting she left him in her will, is incarcerated for her murder, escapes from prison, flees an assassin – in short, leads a life that is one special-effects, Big Dipper, fast-and-furious, madcap escapade after another. And throughout all of it he never stops talking. Then right at the end, abruptly, he's shot dead, and rigor mortis indeed sets in.

The hotel he manages, however, perched high on a mountain peak in Mitteleuropa, caters exclusively to those who are served and are not busy at all – or at least not while cocooned in the fading opulence of the Grand Budapest. All the same, even the upper crust have to do *something* between getting up in the morning and going to bed at night: eat, drink, read (there's a library), have sex, exchange murmured banalities with each other, loll in a mineral bath, or admire the view. At the very least they might smoke. In summer they presumably also stroll about, braced by the mountain air, occasionally playing some game or other with a ball, but we don't see what happens in summer at the Grand Budapest because all the action takes place in the snowy depths of winter.

Utter idleness seems much less in fashion these days, even at supposedly grand hotels like the Mayfair. Perhaps it's a fading art. It was the same last week on the tea estate, lost in the fog across the valley somewhere. The hotel there is not grand, either, although luxuriously appointed (the bed linen is hand-embroidered, while maids, waiters and gardeners vastly outnumber the guests). Basically it's two large, verandahed tea-planter's bungalows set amongst lawns and lush gardens in the middle of tea estates stretching over an area three times the size of Monaco. It's boutique. My fellow guests were a party of ebullient Dutch tea aficionados, two English widows and a couple from Wimbledon. I was a disappointment to them, I know, I could read it in their eyes, because, like Christopher Robin, I kept trying to do 'Nothing'. They were all out and about in the fog, visiting the tea pickers' villages, touring the factory and trying to walk into Sikkim, Sikkim being just a hop, step and a jump from here. In the case of the Dutch, when not out and about, they were being strenuously convivial. The couple from Wimbledon seemed to be slightly at a loose end, but that's not the same thing at all as idling or doing nothing. According to the manager, Will, a towering Englishman, idleness causes acute anxiety amongst his guests, who have come to the middle of nowhere to stay busy.

In *The Grand Budapest Hotel* only the Dowager Countess manages to do *absolutely* nothing – by lying dead in her coffin. Unless you are dead, doing *rien du tout, nada, niente* is not only practically impossible, but can cause offence. Years ago, suspecting (for good reason) that my own life would be over in the blink of an eye, I decided to fly First Class around the world. If you're pretty sure the ship's going down, why travel steerage? Sitting next to me in the flower-bedecked cabin was a well-known multimillionaire, a laptop and sheaves of business papers spread out on his tray-table to show that even high above the Wimmera, ensconced in sumptuousness, he hadn't a moment to call his own. Indeed, he no doubt *did* have lots of urgent work to do: the livelihoods of thousands, even tens of thousands, of Australians were shaped in those days by the decisions this man made. Eventually, after exchanging a few desultory words about nothing in particular, he explained to me, at some length, since I showed no sign of having recognised him, just how important he was. After twenty minutes or so of one-upmanship, he said, 'And what do you do?' I said, 'Nothing. I don't do anything at all.' He looked as if I'd just hit him with a plank. 'Nothing?' 'No,'

I lied, glancing idly at my in-flight magazine, 'nothing at all.' We hardly spoke again all the way to Singapore. The idea that a man up the front of a plane – a *man*, not just somebody's wife – might do nothing at all was something he clearly found too shockingly out of kilter with his world view even to discuss. A batty English aristocrat might do nothing at all (Trollope's novels are full of people whose sole occupation is to play whist or dress for dinner), but these days the super-rich are not aristocrats but what Trollope calls 'opulent trades-men': they work hard, and get tetchy if you don't. I did more or less nothing for the rest of the flight. It doesn't come naturally.

Even if it's impossible (strictly speaking) before rigor mortis sets in, doing nothing is still worth attempting fairly regularly, and in particular after the hunting, gathering and feasting is over – not killing for fun or eating to fill in time and display your wealth, but genuine hunting, gathering and feasting, or some modern form of them. We call this sort of stab at doing nothing 'idling' or, less admiringly, 'loafing'. The lower orders, along with teenagers, are often said to 'lounge about', but it all amounts to much the same thing.

Idleness and loafing must not on any account be confused with indolence and slothfulness. In humans, indolence and slothfulness are signs of a weak character or adolescence, whereas idleness and loafing can, on the contrary, indicate strength of character, a resolve, a maturity, a firmness of purpose that approaches nobility. Flanders and Swann, for instance, sing of a sloth who lives 'a life of ease / Contented not to do or die, / But idle as I please.' Yes, their sloth *could*, as he muses melodiously, climb the Himalayas, become a champion tennis player, marry a princess, play the clarinet, paint a Mona Lisa or 'be another Caesar', but he prefers to 'sleep and dream and doze'. In other words, their sloth is not slothful at all, he is an idler. Hanging upside down doing as little as possible isn't simply part of their sloth's nature, but something he has *chosen* to do, as have all genuine idlers and loafers. This is crucial: in doing virtually nothing, idlers are exercising dominion over time. Mind you, there's a tendency for both the bourgeoisie and those who own land or the means of production to label anyone who refuses to integrate his or her leisure into a productive network of some kind as 'slothful'. They will certainly see lying in a hammock in the sun as slothful (or lazy or indolent), but might feel equally censorious of reading poetry, walking the dog or learning Ancient Greek for the sheer joy of it. On the other hand, leisure activities such as jogging, listening to music or renovating the kitchen will put money in somebody's pocket (no, not yours), so won't be construed as slothful. It's a misuse of the word 'sloth'.

But how best to idle? What are the loafer's or idler's real choices in the twenty-first century?

In earlier centuries the leisured classes had servants to do what had to be done to keep a family comfortably housed, clothed and fed – to do the work, in other words – so were free much of the time to enjoy themselves in whatever way took their fancy. Goncharov's Oblomov, for instance, a nobleman in his early thirties in 1850s St Petersburg and poster-boy of layabouts everywhere for over 150 years, spends most of his day every day in a trance-like state, lying on his sofa in his iconic dressing-gown – *by choice*. That's his reaction to the pointlessness of existence for men of his class. Now and again a friend or passing scrounger might drop in to harangue him or cadge a meal, or he might half-read a book or think about going to Paris, but mostly he just lies there doing nothing, half-asleep, imagining. He has a cantankerous but devoted servant, Zakhar, to feed and dress him, and an overseer to manage his serfs and run his estate in the country. His young friend Volkov, on the other hand, who drops in to see him when he has nothing better to do, enjoys an 'endless social round', with visits to the Vyaznikovs on Sundays, Prince Tyumenev on Wednesdays, the Savinovs on Thursdays, and the Maklashins on Fridays, not to mention the theatre, the opera, the tailor, and the odd *bal champêtre*. He also hunts and takes walks in the woods with whomever he's in love with at the time. The very thought of all this social activity bores Oblomov to death. Doing nothing doesn't bore him, but the thought of 'society' does. 'Society', he tells his German friend Stoltz, with all the 'flitting back and forth like flies' that people seem to do, dancing away their lives and cruising up and down the Nevsky Prospekt just looking at each other, is 'even more asleep than I am'. You know what he means. The idea of falling in love – sex, in other words – perks him up briefly, but not permanently. Oblomov's reaction to life's futility is to fail to get up.

In England, as we know from Trollope, the gentry also enjoyed hunting and courting, as well as dining, playing cards at the club, reading, meeting friends to discuss sex and money, and occasionally travelling. Travel is one of the well-established ways the idle seek to kill time: they smoke, drink, drug themselves and travel. It never quite works.

The real-life Sitwells, I read recently, who have been landowners in north Derbyshire for centuries, also indulged in riding to hounds, shooting, fishing, holding balls, marrying and, in more recent times, playing golf, which markets itself as one of the more refined versions of doing nothing. Golf is doing nothing along with other people – nice people. Of course, the Sitwells also made music and famously collected things: they collected books, furniture and paintings, turning Renishaw Hall, set amongst its renowned Italianate gardens, into one of England's great houses. They also collected talented young men and women – William Walton, for example. Sir George Sitwell, father of Edith, Osbert and Sacheverell, I seem to remember, also invented . . . was it a musical toothbrush? Certainly he came up with a very small revolver for shooting wasps. A stab at creativity, however feeble, is always a boon.

Nowadays, in our sort of society, almost nobody is gentry, even the gentry these days is trade, and almost nobody is free 'much of the time' – in fact, everyone makes a point of not being. Here at the Mayfair I am totally free, since I'm playing at being gentry of the old-fashioned kind, to all intents and purposes starring in my own costume drama. Back at the tea garden, though, I suspect that only the English widows amongst the guests were free to enjoy themselves in whatever way took their fancy. The couple from Wimbledon, despite in effect having servants to take care of their every need, seemed anxious about having time on their hands and kept trying to think of things to do, while for the Dutch tea connoisseurs their stay on the estate was about as relaxed as a military manoeuvre. Of course, it was the Dutch who first brought tea to Europe, so we must make allowances for their zeal.

So, what in the early twenty-first century are the real choices?

Notionally, at one extreme you have immobility with an empty mind. In an era of constant noise and messaging – billboards, television, radio, cyberspace, smartphones – radical disengagement and an empty mind can seem attractive. I don't mean the kind of somnolent reverie that Oblomov lay sunk in – Oblomov *thought*, he *imagined*, he *felt*; empty was precisely what his mind was not. His listlessness was hardly commendable, but his torpor, Goncharov tells us, even had a kind of grace, his squalid room (Zakhar being as lazy as he was) an air of 'cloistered calm'.

No, I mean the sort of immobility with an empty mind now marketed as 'stillness', an evocative word that can mean both quiet and being at rest. People have started busily writing books about stillness, organising courses on it, taking classes in it, and fanning out across the globe to find places to be still in. A Canadian woman in the row behind me on the plane north from Calcutta a few days ago never stopped talking about stillness. Leonard Cohen, I gathered from a book on the subject by Pico Iyer, sat 'stock-still' for a week at a time. Here in the shadow of the Kanchenjunga range, within cooee of Tibet, the hills are alive with Europeans and Americans seeking stillness. What is meant by this word is hard to pin down: it seems to mean everything from taking a break from busyness to think about what you've been busy doing ('stepping away now and then so that you can see the world more clearly and love it more deeply', as Iyer puts it, with a seductive sentimental flourish you really have to be American to fall for), to Keats's 'drowsy noons, / And evenings steep'd in honey'd indolence'; from hyper-alertness while doing nothing, to a version of *sahaja* (a Sanskrit word implying effortless being); from narcissistic self-communing, to a dry run for Nirvana itself. Like love, it seems to mean whatever you can afford. On the back of Pico Iyer's book it's summed up neatly: 'sitting quietly in a room might be the ultimate adventure'. Precisely.

To me, immobility with an empty mind actually sounds like an extreme form of solipsism and boredom – pure boredom, as it were, not just acute boredom, but pure, Schopenhauerian boredom. 'What is boredom but the feeling of the emptiness of life?' Schopenhauer wrote (inaccurately, but with feeling). In fact, some might claim it's so pure that it's not *even* boredom in the traditional sense: true boredom has a whiff of longing about it, surely, an undertone of ennui, a niggling awareness of what one could or should be doing instead of what one is actually doing, a faint consciousness, at a time of utter plotlessness, of plausible plot-lines if only things were not as they are, if only one could escape (the meeting, the sermon, the motel room, the prison cell). Chekhov's Three Sisters, for instance, bored beyond endurance in the provinces, yearn for Moscow; Richmal

Crompton's William, the little boy I'd have loved to be, dreams when bored of new ways to get hold of sixpence, or to outsmart girls or farmers or that shifty-eyed, stuck-up Hubert Lane; and virtually every bored adult contemplates a sexual escapade, even if they call it love or marriage – well, it's the only vivifying form of social intercourse available to many of us. In other words, immobility with an empty mind, at least in theory, may be beyond boredom. I must admit that I am little drawn to savour it. To me it smacks of the sort of gloomy indifference I find most Buddhist temples and monasteries swathed in – the one just down the road from here at Ghum, for example, hushed and yellow in the grey mist. I tend to see detachment and indifference as the curse of the twentieth century.

In any case, an empty mind is, strictly speaking, an impossibility – that's the whole point of a mind: it thinks things – it pictures, calculates, remembers, makes judgements and decisions, is flooded with sensations. Even an earwig, one presumes, *thinks* – not in the way we do, of course, but in an earwig-ish way. 'What do you think the dog's thinking now?' I often, and pointlessly, wonder aloud. 'Nothing,' my partner Peter says, 'her mind's a blank.' Nonsense. She's aquiver with doggy thoughts twenty-four hours a day – although not with words. Or do certain words indeed detonate in her mind as she lies in front of the fire or walks in the bush – 'dinner', 'wallaby', 'no' and so on? We'll probably never know (although somebody somewhere is no doubt working on finding out).

'Sometimes I sits and thinks,' Winnie-the-Pooh tells us, 'and sometimes I just sits.' But he's a bear. Worse: he's a toy bear. For us humans, if we are sound in mind and body, 'just sitting', without thinking, is scarcely feasible: we have language. (Indeed, tellingly, in the original *Punch* cartoon that Pooh was echoing, it's an uneducated bumpkin with an injured foot, asked by the vicar's wife how on earth a man who can't read or 'get about' occupies his time, who first comes up with the line: 'Well, mum, sometimes I sits and thinks and then again I just sits.' Was the cartoonist laughing at the vicar's wife or at the bumpkin?)

It's true that many Zen practitioners regard words as an encumbrance to pure thought, obstructing the perception of truth. Zen, along with the futon, was one of several aspects of Japanese culture promoted by the Americans after World War II as part of a bulwark against communism. Like the futon, it's starting to look impractical and quaint. Nowadays it's wabi-sabi, rather than Zen, we like to dabble in: nobody is quite sure what it is, it sounds less religious and it fits more comfortably into our suburban lifestyles, approaching nothingness through small things – listening to foghorns in the distance, for example, or crows cawing. Yoga has certainly stayed popular and some yoga practices are also said to be able to overcome the obstacle of language, progressively stemming the torrent of words coursing through our minds until they're finally empty of all their egotistical, coercive prattling: you focus your mind on a simple object or design and, like mist before the sun, the mental chatter begins to die away. Gradually, the infinitesimal becomes the infinite, even (I've seen it claimed) on occasion the Infinite, or possibly both – God, in other words. At this point, eventually, with practice, you should be able to let the object or design you were originally concentrating on fade from your consciousness. Your mind should now be empty and silent. Awareness without thought. Pure being.

I stare into the fog, the wall of nothingness dropping away beneath the hotel, and contemplate this. What in God's name is 'pure being'? It sounds to me like death. Or at the very least foetal. What could be more existentially boring than the infinite? Than infinite anything? (And boredom, after all, even of the pure kind, is an alarm bell just like angina: something is radically wrong!)

Well, I can only speak from my own experience. Over a lifetime I've visited dozens of lamaseries and *gompas*, temples and retreats, from Dharamshala, Ladakh and Sarnath (where Buddha delivered his first sermon) here in India to places much further afield – in Nepal, Sri Lanka, Thailand, Japan and . . . now my own mind is misting over and I can barely place them all. Korea, perhaps? Wollongong? Nowhere have I seen the slightest evidence of emptiness, let alone of wordlessness. I've gazed at countless images and statues of Buddha and myriad bodhisattvas meditating. I've listened to priests chanting by the hundreds, I've looked into their eyes as they practise mindfulness. Whatever they're supposed to be doing, unless they're in a coma, they have to be thinking. There may indeed be a welcome lull in the chatter – how can anyone know? – but so what? It will come back. Let's hope so, anyway!

No, at the core of our era's nihilism, the nausea gripping Europeans by the throat, lies precisely a loss of authentic contact with the finite people and objects surrounding us. Commotion is certainly a problem in big cities – I'm fresh from Calcutta, I know all about commotion – but a far greater problem, surely, is detachment. (Dostoyevsky, Chekhov, Sartre, Camus and André Gide are all good on this subject. So is Alberto Moravia, come to think of it. Speaking of whom: there's a slim Moravia I've never read before on the coffee table in the Mayfair's library.)

Being aware of awareness and nothing else, as some of his followers have suggested Siddhartha Gautama was, has no meaning I can pin down: it's one of those formulae, like the notion of formlessness, that makes you feel quite spiritual when you say it to yourself, or at least drowsy, but actually refers to nothing that is known to happen in the existing universe. The historical Siddhartha Gautama's mind must have in fact swarmed with Magadhi Prakrit words until the instant when, exactly like the Dowager Countess Céline Villeneuve Desgoffe und Taxis, he did indeed achieve formlessness by ceasing to exist in the space–time continuum. You might think in smells, colours, melodies, pictures or mandalas, you might even in short bursts meditate on infinite consciousness turning into infinite nothingness, but not for long: words will soon start forming in your mind and sticking to things in time and space because you are a speaking animal. Many of us dream of other possibilities, but, as far as the human species collectively knows, that is what you are and all you are. One of the signs of boredom in the brains of the dangerously bored is the isolation of the language-processing centre from other areas of the brain – the dying down of crosstalk, as Peter Toohey calls it in his scintillating study of boredom (*Boredom: A Lively History*). How could I forget that phrase? In healthy humans the language centre keeps humming. Escaping from language into lasting wordlessness would be dangerous and is ultimately impossible. Intervals of silence are one thing, wordlessness quite another. I can see why the streets of Dharamshala and Varanasi are positively thrumming with the robed devotees of these practices gabbling away on their mobile phones and congregating in loud groups on street corners and in restaurants, floating on clouds of words. They are alive with words, these men (and here they are men), their minds and ears hungry for words after the silence.

All the same, you can see the attraction of immobility with an empty mind for leisure-seekers: it's one of the purest forms of doing absolutely nothing that humans have ever devised, and after a bit of frenetic hunting and eating, what could seem more blissful? It doesn't have to be aimed at achieving Buddhahood, supreme self-realisation doesn't have to be on the menu, it can just be a pleasant, half-asleep sort of thing to do. I've seen it referred to by one cynic as 'religious loafing'. But who needs the religion bit? My partner, an ardent atheist, does it to help him cope with fear of flying. I'm conscious that all over the globe at this very instant, as I loll here dreaming of Kanchenjunga appearing on the horizon, tens of thousands, perhaps hundreds of thousands, even millions of people are choosing to sit and meditate. (Standing up also works powerfully, it's claimed, if the body is properly aligned, but sitting, even on a chair, seems to promote a nice mixture of relaxation and concentrated thought. Understandably, lying down is not recommended for the beginner.) And meditation may well be as life-enhancing as it claims to be, too, every bit as efficacious as fish oil or aspirin, if more bother. In fact, I'd be astounded if neurologists at the University of California or East Anglia haven't conclusively proved it is. Or have researchers at the University of Minnesota conclusively proved it isn't?

Either way, leisure is not about promoting a healthy mind in a healthy body. Leisure is about pleasure. *Leisure is an end in itself.*

Speaking of meditating lying down, what could be more delicious than seeing how close you can come to doing absolutely nothing by taking a short nap? It's especially delectable in the heat of the day in the tropics, where you can shamelessly nap (or slumber or snooze or zizz or get a bit of kip) with the doors and windows open, or even in the street. Exactly how pleasurable it is, though, rather depends on what you were doing before dozing off. According to the Spanish maxim, 'It's sweet to do nothing for a while and then have a little rest.' But that's just amiable nonsense, surely. It's only seriously sweet if you've been working – it's much less sweet if you're a grandee (a member of the aristocracy unacquainted from birth with labour – less sweet for Oblomov, for instance, than for his man Zakhar) and not sweet at all if you're unemployed. To be frank, I enjoyed my half-hour of shut-eye much less after lunch today than at home because here I'm not working, I'm pretending to be a prince. To be truly sweet, Jerome K. Jerome believed, idleness must be stolen. In other words, idling can't be fully enjoyed unless you have plenty of work to do. There's no fun, as he famously quipped, in doing nothing when you have nothing to do because in that case 'wasting time' becomes more or less your occupation. *Il dolce far niente* must never be that: it must always be something you consciously settle on doing.

Take sleeping in: dispiriting for the jobless, but reinvigorating for everyone else. Should I get up now, you might say to yourself when the alarm goes off (especially on a weekday), have breakfast and then do a spot of work? How much pleasanter to cock a snook at the day's demands, as Oblomov did. 'The moment he got up in the morning,' Goncharov writes of Oblomov,

> he would drink his tea and then straight away lie down on the divan, propping his head up on his hand and thinking about everything with remorseless intensity until finally his head felt tired from working so hard and his conscience told him that he had done enough for one day for the common good. Free now from workaday concerns, he loved to retreat into himself and live in a world of his own creation.

Delicious. Lazy by nature he may be, coming as he does from a long line of gentlefolk who spend half their lives asleep, as well as disinclined to engage with the empty-headed world beyond his apartment, sunk in meaningless toing and froing, but he claims that he's stopped working and stays all day half-dressed on the sofa in order to 'live', not to rest: 'When am I supposed to live?' he asks (himself). Not while working, clearly. Who can live while working? So he stops. He goes too far, I'll concede that: he turns his whole life into a siesta.

So does a character – is it Byrne? – in that phantasmagorical work of genius *At Swim-Two-Birds* by the Irishman Flann O'Brien that Peter was reading compulsively just before I left home. Byrne claims that what's wrong with most people is that they don't spend sufficient time in bed. Our conception of repose and activity, he says, must be turned upside down. 'We should not sleep to recover the energy expended when awake but rather wake occasionally to defecate the unwanted energy that sleep engenders.' A five-mile race at full tilt around the town should do it, he opines, and then back to bed and the arms of Morpheus. 'You're a terrible man for the blankets, said Kerrigan.' Indeed.

If you are going to lie in, it's important to assume the right posture. As Confucius said millennia ago, never lie stretched out straight in bed like a corpse. Lin Yutang recommends two basic postures: curled up on your side or lying back in a pile of soft pillows at an angle of thirty degrees. He knew what he was talking about.

For some reason, though, sleeping in makes most people feel guilty – 'bed-guilt' Tom Hodgkinson calls

it in his popular manifesto *How to Be Idle*, blaming
Christianity in general and Protestantism in particular
for this sense of sin. G. K. Chesterton, who was a
champion of lying in bed and an ardent Roman
Catholic, blames the modern tendency when passing
moral judgement to inflate 'very small and secondary
matters of conduct' at the expense of 'very great and
primary ones' (adultery, I presume he means, and
burglary). If you ask those who are diffident about
lying in bed why they feel guilty, they usually smile
sheepishly and tell you that they feel they'd be 'wasting
time' if they slept in. What on earth can this mean?
Time is time: you spend it freely or you spend it in
bondage, with an eye to your needs and what you owe
others. Do they mean, for example, that on a Saturday
when their time is theoretically their own they should
get up and answer a few emails, recharge the mobile,
ring their mother, brush the dog, mow the lawn, drive
the kids to tennis, stick on a load of washing, plant out
the seedlings they bought yesterday before they wilt,
and stew some fruit? Or on a Sunday should they be
sitting in the sun with a coffee, perusing the papers? Or
even going to church? (*Should, should, should. Ought,
must, have to.*) Well, the true idler will mutter into the
pillow, I'm not going to, I'm going to roll over and
drift off again, I'm going to stay in bed this morning
and snooze, I'm going to taste what Hodgkinson calls

'the nectar of oblivion'. (I'm not sure that 'oblivion' is the right word – it sounds a bit like nothingness – but 'nectar' is perfect.)

In a word, sleeping in must always be an assertion of your right to loaf, the very embodiment of your self-mastery, as dozing straight after lunch should be (the time-honoured hour for snoozing, as natural as hunting with the pack). It should never be *mere* torpor. A dandyish touch is one thing, but simply failing to get up quite another.

It also behoves all of us, surely, to acknowledge that *somebody* has to get up *somewhere*. This is something that Tom Hodgkinson fails to do in *How to Be Idle*. You can only lie in habitually if somebody else habitually gets up early, as they once did in the houses of the gentry. Few of Tom Hodgkinson's readers will be gentry any more than he is.

The siesta is a different kettle of fish from sleeping in. Far from embodying torpor, the siesta, I would argue, along with loitering, underpins the imaginative life, and civilisation cannot exist without it. Without the siesta, all you have is shop-keeping.

Even the dogs at Oblomovka, Oblomov's home village, took a siesta after the midday meal, since there was nobody left to bark at. At Oblomovka everyone took the siesta very seriously indeed.

It was an all-engulfing, all-defeating slumber, truly like death itself. Everything was dead apart from cacophonous snoring of every kind coming from every corner of the house. Once in a while someone would lift a sleepy head and look about, surprised and uncomprehending, in both directions, turn onto the other side or, with eyes still closed and half-asleep, spit, and then, with a smacking of the lips or muttering something to himself, fall asleep again.

Someone else would suddenly and without any preliminary measures spring to his feet from where he was lying, as if fearing to waste precious minutes, grab a mug of kvass and blow the flies that were floating in it to the other rim. Motionless up until that point, the flies would now start to stir in the hope of improving their situation. The sleeper would wet his throat and then fall back onto the bed as if someone had shot him.

I first surrendered to the pleasures of the siesta as an alternative to work when I was an undergraduate student with a regular French class at two o'clock in the afternoon. In those days nuns still wore wimples – or at least Sister Mary Joseph and Sister Carmel McNulty did. There was quite a bit of competition in the two o'clock class for a seat directly behind them. If you were lucky, by two-fifteen, when Professor B.'s voice was becoming little more than a distant drone at the front of the room ('*Considérons alors . . . Blaise Pascal, au contraire . . . En revanche . . .*'), you could safely lower your head to the desk and fall fast asleep. It was bliss because in those long-gone days of wimples we had a midday meal. We didn't just gobble down a cheese and tomato sandwich and call it lunch, there was no slapdash snacking on the run in the sixties, coffee in a polystyrene cup in one hand, a lukewarm pasty in the other: no, in those days we had a proper lunch. And after lunch you needed to *faire une sieste*. And, *en plus*, the room where Professor B. delivered his lectures was stuffy and warm, even in winter, with windows facing north to catch the sun. Half the class was desperate for a nun. At about two-forty-five I would drift back into consciousness, sit up, look around and start to take a renewed interest in the world, although rarely in what Professor B. had to say – on a Tuesday afternoon in spring in Canberra who cares about Jansenism? About depravity possibly, but not what Jansenists thought about it. I'd just had a little nap. It was like a blessing. All listlessness has evaporated, I would think to myself, I am a new man.

And now, decades later, all wimples gone from the world, and seventeenth-century French literature itself offered for study very sparsely around the globe, I still take a daily siesta. I take one at home, I take one when travelling. I took one today here in this nest of would-be gentlefolk and their servants in West Bengal. At home I am without fail companionably joined for my siesta by my dog, who stops whatever she's been doing (including nothing), makes sure I'm supine in the right recliner, in the right position with the right rug across my legs, sighs deeply and then, like the dogs in Oblomovka, takes a nap with me, snoring heavily. This is a foretaste of heaven.

The siesta, even more than rolling over and going back to sleep, represents 'freedom and self-mastery', according to the French philosopher Thierry Paquot, and that is, after all, the very essence of leisure. In fact, if Paquot is to be believed, it represents 'a high point in [the] art of living', which is perhaps going a little too far, but Paquot is a philosopher of urbanism, a specialist in the field, and his fundamental point, I gather from his book *The Art of the Siesta*, is really that for the city-dweller it's vital to find a way to escape from the city's natural tendency to organise, restrict, package up (and sometimes sell on) our lives – and the siesta is one way to do precisely that. The siesta is the city-dweller's 'act of resistance', being 'truly free time, belonging to no-one but the person who takes it'. You can catnap for ten minutes, or two hours, you can nod off on a bus, in a mosque, at the beach, in a deckchair in the garden, or on a bed beside a friend. To do so represents an enlivening rhythm, not habit. (We must not mistake rhythm for habit.) It is a stab at enjoying the incomplete, the uncertain, the haphazard, the unstable, the risky and the imperfect, all endangered in the modern city. Its hush is a hiatus in the hubbub of city living, respite from the mills, the markets, the roads, the trains, the tyranny (Paquot would say) of the world of *market* value. Mind you, I also enjoy taking a siesta in the country.

Who has captured the voluptuousness of the siesta better than the French poet José-Maria de Hérédia? His half-closed eyelids, 'languid with sleep', are laced with flashes of vermilion, his eyes aswarm with 'richly coloured butterflies grown drunk upon the light'.

> It's then that my trembling fingers seize each thread of light
> And in the golden mesh of this faint, subtly woven net,
> A peaceful hunter, I now snare my dreams.

Too lush? Well, he *was* born in Cuba, and was a staunch Parnassian (art for art's sake, beauty above all things), so was the natural prey of the demons of the sixth hour (the Roman noon – the *sexta hora, la siesta*). The Romans lunched early, much earlier than we do, before the sun was at its zenith, then hid from the madness – the ghosts, the Midday Fiend, the lascivious succubi – stalking the shadowless streets, and had a little lie-down in the dark. Masturbation was popular, according to Monsieur Paquot, during this collective drawing of breath, particularly amongst goatherds, although not cowherds, and, as happens today in countries where the siesta is popular, copulation commonly occurred before or after the surrender to sleep. In other words, during the sixth hour a brief 'derangement of the senses' was de rigueur long before Rimbaud thought of it as a way for somebody to study his own – or even her own – soul.

On waking from a siesta you drink tea. I have no idea what the Romans drank – a spot of honeyed wine? – but nowadays, right across the civilised world, you drink tea. Tea-drinking is one of the most refined ways we have of moving gently from doing nothing to doing something. At Oblomovka, for instance, two hundred years ago, a man came running from the kitchen carrying a huge samovar, whereupon, yawning, scratching their heads and clearing their parched throats, everyone would gather, bleary-eyed and looking crumpled, to drink tea. Up to twelve cups sometimes – Russians love their tea, they've been drinking tea almost as long as the Dutch have, but originally got it directly from the Chinese, unlike the French and British. At our place tea is also customary when we get up after our siesta. Coffee would be quite out of place: coffee, as Hodgkinson has noted, is for workers; tea is for those he calls intellectuals.

Tea is drunk languidly, tea never hurries you, tea is 'poised', as they say up here in Darjeeling, encouraging introspection, refreshing gradually, with a kind of delicacy, even tenderness (according to a Japanese book I've been dipping into in the library) that coffee doesn't aspire to. One drinks tea, the Chinese sage T'ien Yiheng reflected centuries ago, 'to forget the world's noise. It is not for those who eat rich food and dress in silk pyjamas.' The Japanese connoisseur Kakuzo Okakura closer to our own time called tea piquant but charming. Tea was apparently popular in Japan for warding off drowsiness during long hours of Buddhist meditation. Tea, in a word, is a polite amusement, while coffee is for jolting workers into action. Tellingly, coffee often comes in 'shots'. These days the streets around our city centres are full of workers (builders, shopgirls, bank clerks) heading back to the office or building site with a cup of tepid coffee held out in front of them like a bunch of flowers or a pathology specimen. If you must drink coffee, I suggest you sit over it somewhere. It's the sitting, not the drinking, that the idler should aspire to.

It must be after three – I wouldn't mind another cup of tea myself. I spot Shubham. He flashes me a brilliant smile and hurries over to see what it is I might like. He's from somewhere down on the plains near Varanasi. Assam with milk? Darjeeling Second Flush? Oolong? And would I like a biscuit? Yes, please. Shortbread? Perfect – hardly local, but perfect nonetheless.

I don't know about Scottish shortbreads, but tea is, of course, the product of back-breaking toil for next to nothing – on the slopes beneath the Mayfair and all the way northwards into Sikkim for a daily wage of less than

I pay for one cup of it at the café around the corner from where I live. Or will pay for the pot that Shubham brings me, for that matter, here at the Mayfair, where all the guests are pretending to be gentlefolk.

Is the fog thinning at last? Is that actually *sun* I can see out there on the rhododendrons? 'The afternoon glow is brightening the bamboos,' Mr Okakura writes, 'the fountains are bubbling with delight, the soughing of the pines is heard in our kettle. Let us dream of evanescence, and linger in the beautiful foolishness of things.' How Tao. Yes, let's.

'Is the fog lifting, Shubham, do you think?' I ask him when he comes back with the teapot, cup and biscuit, more for something to say than in any expectation that he'll know. 'Would Kanchenjunga be visible if I ducked up to the Mall Road?'

'No,' he says, still beaming, 'not visible.'

'When do you think the fog will lift?'

'Who can say?'

Who indeed.

The trouble with fog is that it really needs framing to be pleasurable. We're simply engulfed in it. Gazing out into its thick, hushed drifts, I know I should try to follow Mr Okakura's advice and accept the fog's invitation to use my imagination about what is out there. Beauty, he keeps telling me, sounding oddly like my French friend Thierry Paquot on the subject of the siesta, is discovered in the play of the imagination faced with imperfection, not in perfection; in the act of completing, not completion.

I can see what he means, but I would still like the fog to lift.

Doing nothing and something at the same time

Is it a good moment to write up my diary? A short chat with myself about what I've been doing today, a page or two of leisurely banter with myself about my aperçus, my stabs at adventure and happenings of little consequence, is the ideal way to do pretty much nothing, yet undeniably something at the same time. Or would I be better off sitting for a while in my room or the library with a good book? The Anita Brookner, perhaps? Before her husband dies, and not needing to work, the heroine of *The Rules of Engagement*, Elizabeth Wetherall, leads a life of 'benign numbness', punctuated by shopping and preparing meals, a state she mistakes for contentment. Once he's dead, however, she is at a loss for something to do, so she spends most mornings reading in a café to fill in time: a comfortably-off middle-class woman who finished school will naturally think first of reading.

Was Dionysus at a loss for something to do when he picked up Euripides' *Andromeda* to read for a bit of shipboard recreation? It's unlikely: he was the god of wine and ritual madness. His comments on the play in another Greek classic (Aristophanes' *Frogs*) are apparently the first reference we have to somebody reading alone for the sheer pleasure of it – sexual pleasure, according to his half-brother Heracles, but Dionysus denies it. He says his pleasure was mostly culinary. How modern. Whatever the case, I doubt he was reading to relieve an inner numbness.

I don't think I read recreationally to keep numbness at bay, either – to restore a certain freshness to the way I see the world, perhaps, to sharpen my sensibilities, but not simply as an antidote to numbness. I only rarely read these days to redeem my humanity, see the world through others' eyes or even to improve my mind. Sometimes I dare say I read for the high-minded reason the Japanese poet Kenkō read seven hundred years ago: for the sense of 'hold[ing] intimate converse with men of unseen generations' – or even my own generation, intimacy and conversation with the nonchalantly wise being two of life's principle pleasures, as far as I'm concerned. In a more modern stab at high seriousness, the Venetian detective Commissario Brunetti in one of Donna Leon's recent novels declares that if you rid the world of books you'd wipe out memory. You wouldn't, of course, but there's an echo of Kenkō's 'converse with men of unseen generations' here that is seductive. The detective's wife is an even more ardent champion of books than he is: if you rid the world of books, according to Paola, you'd destroy culture, ethics and the multitude of opinions and arguments at variance with your own ideas. Hardly, but her enthusiasm is heartwarming, especially given that she's Italian: as the writer Dacia Maraini once explained to me, Italians don't read at all, they just write.

Nearly two thousand years ago in ancient Oxyrhynchus, the Egyptian City of the Sharp-Nosed Fish whose rubbish dump has recently been excavated, the inhabitants were no less enthusiastic about reading than the Brunettis. From the papyri it's clear that they read for fun as well as to broaden their minds. Just as we do now, they scrolled down for housekeeping tips, amorous techniques, health advice and a choice of magic spells. Anything touching on the interpretation of dreams was popular, too. They read Homer, the Christian gospels (stirring stuff about little guys sticking it up the Romans), Greek philosophy, biographies of the famous and fiction of a seriously sensational, and even racy, kind. (Novels are nothing new, either – why do we imagine they are?) This appears to have been intelligent leisure reading of an astoundingly modern kind.

I mostly read these days, I suspect, in order to do nothing and something at the same time – to have adventures without moving an inch. To invade Tibet with Lieutenant Colonel Sir Francis Younghusband, for instance (and also, like him, establish my own religion), to cross Borneo on foot with Redmond O'Hanlon (who admits to being unhinged), or to cross Europe on foot with Patrick Leigh Fermor (who definitely was not). I read in order to . . . I was going to say 'to be many people', but perhaps it would be more accurate to say 'to be more multifariously myself' – more daringly, more colourfully, more honestly, more cannily, more deeply, more many-sidedly myself. (Is that, however, verging on the high-minded?) I rarely read recent fiction these days, for reasons I don't quite understand. I certainly make no attempt to 'keep up'.

Instead of reading, many people think you'd be better off getting out into the world more often. Robert Louis Stevenson, I seem to remember, calls it a 'mighty bloodless substitute for life' (in a book of his). A reader, he says, resembles the Lady of Shalott, sitting yearningly, despairingly in her tower, with her back turned on all the bustle and glamour of reality, looking at the world, and Sir Lancelot, in her mirror. But can't you do both? Read and live? When the Lady of Shalott did escape her tower to pursue Sir Lancelot, Mr Stevenson, she actually froze to death.

Reading is at least more involving than going to the cinema because it asks so much more of the imagination.

A well-exercised imagination is what makes a day seem like a thousand years. 'I feel more and more every day,' Keats wrote to his brother George, 'as my imagination strengthens, that I do not live in this world alone but in a thousand worlds . . .' I am not Keats, I do not live every day in a thousand worlds. I long to live in a thousand worlds, yet all the same I am and am also not, for instance, Sebastian Flyte in *Brideshead Revisited*; I am and am also not Elizabeth Wetherall; I am and am also not Ilya Ilyich Oblomov; and I very much am and am very much not the adolescent boy in Alberto Moravia's *Agostino* (which I've just chanced upon) – he's me, he's all my friends from school when we were fourteen, and he's also no more me or any of my friends from school than Mussolini was. Reading is like shaking the kaleidoscope of who you are: the shards in there are the same old shards, but something reconfigures them. You feel new, you feel rediscovered. You feel freed from the prison of your everyday self. Reading really is, after all, a brilliant way to do nothing and something at the same time.

There must be other ways to do this sitting down, and, to be honest, I'm in the mood for doing something a little more mischievous than reading, as one often is on vacation, but it's hard to think of what. I could turn on the television, I suppose. Like going to see *The Grand Budapest Hotel* on Good Friday, watching television during daylight hours is faintly wicked, but is it wicked enough? It's often seen as doing both something and nothing at the same time, exactly like reading a good book, or listening to good music, or even, in the right company (I am constantly assured), playing golf. But it's not, really. Watching television is almost always a matter of doing absolutely nothing, neither the body nor the mind being engaged, like scrolling through social media feeds on a mobile phone. At root it's indolence, not idleness; it's being vapidly entertained while shopping. Very occasionally a good television program (a documentary about meerkats, say, a spiffing slice of Nordic noir or a bit of social satire – *A Moody Christmas*, for instance) might give you a real sense of doing something and nothing at the same time – indeed, that's how you know it's good – but not often. David Attenborough is usually far too earnest. I must say Brian Cox on the cosmos and the meaning of everything strikes a good balance as a rule: hunky with just a touch of Flopsy Bunny yet full of wildly interesting information. On the whole, though, watching television is a last resort.

In picturing Brian Cox I am reminded: at a good concert, I regularly have the sensation of not just doing something small and expected (sitting silent and immobile in my seat, eyes fixed on the musicians), but simultaneously of doing something vast, something inexpressibly beautiful and all-encompassing, not unlike time-travelling across the cosmos. It can be profoundly calming, but also at other times hair-raisingly exciting.

At the hotel I stay at in Varanasi, every evening during dinner on the terrace, sitting cross-legged on a low divan, a man in late middle age plucks a sitar while his much younger companion (dark skin gleaming in the candle-light) plays the tablas, head thrown back in ecstasy as he drums. I know nothing about Indian music – I can float on it for hours, but know nothing about it at all – yet I know that this music is good precisely because every evening as I listen, I have found myself effortlessly doing both nothing and something marvellous at the same time. 'Do you like our music?' the younger man calls out after each offering. 'Yes,' we all call back, 'we like it *very* much,' not knowing why we like it, but knowing we do. At some level, of course, what we like is less the music than ourselves floating on it.

At this hour alone at the Mayfair in the fog, I can't think of anything wayward to indulge in at all while lounging about. A spot of Anita Brookner on the bed will have to do.

⌒

Once upon a time there was smoking, of course, but that's completely out of the question. Smoking is so exquisitely unsatisfying, as Oscar Wilde remarked, the epitome of gauzy, gypsyish *fainéantise*, of languor shot through with a zest for living – but nowadays (quite understandably) it's a pastime that's frowned upon, even at the Mayfair. Slaughtering innocent creatures and eating them is not frowned upon at all, but smoking is. Professor André Spicer from the University of Warwick, an international expert on organisational stupidity, blames the drastic decline in smoking, along with the use of smartphones, for depriving modern Westerners of 'thinking time', leaving us markedly more stupid than we need to be. The 'five-minute little break we used to have' a couple of dozen times a day, doing nothing but thinking, he says, led to better informed debate, better organisational decisions and 'a far better public life'. In fine weather, he arranges two 'pop-up philosophy chairs', as he calls them – two deckchairs – in front of 'stupidity-intensive' buildings such as the Houses of Parliament in London to give passers-by a place to sit for a moment and simply think – but, alas! not to smoke. That would be a scandalous step too far.

This would be the ideal moment for savouring a cigarette – not a pipe or cigar (which with all their paraphernalia, their pouches and cigar-cutters and smoking-chairs, fail to be evanescent, as the moment itself is), but a slim, white, papery cigarette. At this point in the afternoon, time needs killing, artfully. Nothing, as cigarette-smokers know, produces quite the tiny rush of infinity to break up time that a cigarette does. It doesn't last, it's over almost before it started, time resumes, but that's why it's perfect. It is, as about a third of the world's adult population knew until quite recently, an incomparable way to not work – to do something for the pure pleasure of it, not for profit (yours or your master's). 'I do not wish to work,' Guillaume Apollinaire declared, 'I wish to smoke.' He wants to be master of his own time. (There's been something very French about smoking ever since the Spaniards gave them a chance to do it.)

But it's not a pleasure I can permit myself, here at the Mayfair or anywhere else. I'm glad I once did, though. It's the only pleasure we have – the only *volupté*, as the French have put it more descriptively – that the Romans never knew.

It's a dangerous pleasure, obviously, killing many people early. Well, lots of leisure activities kill people early – mountain-climbing, Sunday driving, sunbaking – but in today's world, where for billions of people longevity (human longevity, that is, not a cow's or pig's) is not just important but an absolute value, doing anything likely to kill you early is particularly reprehensible. Smoking seems so preventable, too, and at some level so immoral, so at odds with finer feelings, that we may as well clamp down on it. I agree.

In preventing it, though, the health crusaders and pleasure police would do well to acknowledge that it is the very dangerousness that makes cigarette-smoking so sublime. To light a cigarette is to stand on the edge of a chasm: that's why you do it. Eating chips fried in vegetable oil is also bad for your health, but it's not sublime. Cigarettes are *bad*: that's the point. Like your very being, each one is unexceptional, marked by anguish and soon stubbed out. When you stop smoking, as Sartre, who stopped often, observed, life is a little less worth living. If you want people to stop, you need to take this into account.

∽

If Brookner's heroine, Elizabeth Wetherall, smoked, her idleness might not seem so annoyingly nebulous, so vapid. In fact, having just spent an hour or so in her company, I'm getting slightly cross with her. Even before she was widowed, only sex with her lover seemed to give her any joy; without the prospect of seeing him she couldn't even take a walk around London with any sense of purpose. 'I was reduced to pure vagrancy,' she says.

Vagrancy, a spot of *vagabondage*. Should I perhaps take a walk before darkness falls? Or I could just go out onto the terrace and look.

Just looking is another richly satisfying, yet much underrated way to do more or less nothing, but not quite. Like sipping tea, it's a step up from meditation or slumbering, but a small one. You can walk and look, as the inhabitants of Oblomovka do after their cups of tea, usually beside the river, or you can just look. You can look *at* something and consider it mindfully, if you wish – a cloud, a glinting earring, even Dorset flashing past, say, all spiky with church steeples, if you're on your way to Lyme Regis by train – or, with practice, you can just look. In the plane on the way to India, for instance, I just looked down for an hour at the endless stretches of saltpans and desert in the redness north-west of Oodnadatta. I'm in the mood to just look now, but is there enough to look at in the fog? Fog might be better for listening in.

Russians, interestingly enough, have a whole vocabulary for idly looking – for simply sitting or standing about aimlessly with their eyes open, content to let them rest on whatever they like. And they have lots of words for the sort of people (men, mostly) who do it, some of which (*zeváka, rotozéy, razínya*) imply an open mouth – in other words, gaping when you should be getting on with things. There's a hint of the dunderhead about these words, but nothing more sinister than that. Are Russians simply more adept at gazing and gaping (while still not gawping) than we are? They do it both seated and on their feet all over the country all the time, as any summer visitor will have observed: on embankments and esplanades, in parks and on street corners, at railway stations, and, during the colder months, in shopping arcades. Russians are happy just to look – they *glazeyut* for hours without a qualm. It's best done while leaning against something, but leaning well is an art and not everyone has a flair for it, even in sultrier climes, let alone in Russia.

In Western countries this sort of lounging around with your eyes open is less socially acceptable, particularly in an urban setting amongst the gainfully employed. Staring into the fire at home or on a camping trip arouses few suspicions, nor does staring at water or the sky. However, in a city setting, aimless looking, like aimless dawdling, makes people wonder what you're up to. Observing can be mistaken for reconnoitring. A man on a street corner, leaning back just looking, arouses distrust. (A woman is unlikely to do it in the first place.) An older man or woman might get away with it on a park bench for half an hour or so, but that's because older people are known to be often at a loose end and, in most cases, harmless – for a start, they can't run.

Where I live, if it's warm enough there's usually quite a sprinkling of youngish men in the pedestrian mall in town just standing about looking, surreptitiously smoking and keeping an eye open for whatever it is that this sort of youngish man keeps an eye open for. It's hard to think of them as true idlers in this setting, as men who have chosen to stand or sometimes sit there looking for no other reason than that it gives them pleasure. There's not the right languor to their lounging for that. Personally, I always give them a wide berth. For a start, most of them are not staring idly, but watching – they look as if they're on the qui vive. Or if not staring idly, which demands a certain level of concentration, some of them will be staring vacantly, usually at their phones. What are they expecting? Hollywood to call? More likely a text from their dealer (we think to ourselves) or one of their layabout friends. People walking past are uncomfortable about being stared at by them, too. *Why's the one with the shaved head and the nostril-ring looking at me?* His eyes are following you. *Am I being not just looked at but eyed – or even eyed off?* 'Don't stare!' my partner says to me sometimes when we're out in public. Why not? Because, it transpires, in public in our sort of society nice people don't.

In Indian towns and cities, on the other hand, staring is a perfectly acceptable way for males to idly pass the time. People (men and children) stare in hotel foyers, in shopping malls, on pavements, in parks and in markets. In fact, on the main street of some small towns and villages in India nothing much else is going on. The shop-keepers are outside their shops looking at the passers-by, the passers-by are looking in the shop windows and at each other, while half the male population of the place seems to be sitting or standing beside the roadway looking – possibly smoking, and almost certainly chatting in a desultory fashion to a friend or two, but mainly just looking. There's nothing I like more than to saunter along such a street and look right back. I can't do this at home – or at least, not quite like this – without appearing either shifty or saucy. There might be an exchange of banter as I stroll past, one or two of the shopkeepers might try to seduce me into coming inside their shops ('Just for the pleasure of the eyes', as they say – or is that in Morocco?), a few of them might waylay me just to pass the time of day in idle banter, even to flirt for want of anything better to do, to brighten up the day a bit, perhaps, or out of a natural friskiness, or for a bit of sport with a stranger, as a dog might chase a seagull simply because it's there – but at root all of us, shopkeepers and passers-by, are just looking. There's buying and selling going on, but by no means only that.

And speaking of 'a bit of sport', in Amit Chaudhuri's recent book *Calcutta: Two Years in the City*, in a passage about a visit he makes to the Forum Mall in Elgin Road (one of India's largest, 'ushering in a revolution in the experience of shopping', according to the internet), he describes the crowds 'spectating' around the escalators. It's not a word I'd ever have thought of using, but I like the way it suggests a show of some kind, makes you think of crowds watching a game. 'Never have I seen,' Chaudhuri writes, in malls in other countries, the number of people I've noticed at South City or the Forum leaning against balconies, studying the lower levels, or the people ascending, apparition-like, on the escalator. It might be a mood that's an offshoot of our weather (with its warmth and torpor) which gives us, childhood onward, a lonely, godlike vantage point on life. I know that to spectate thus on the movements of other people is a deep comfort to the purposeless and the homesick.

I, too, rather like 'spectating'. Here in Darjeeling there is an oddly shaped square down the road from my hotel called Chowrasta or simply The Mall, where people gather to look. It lies across the narrow spur at the top of the town, with alleyways and roadways lined with shops and stalls trailing off down the hill in every direction into the fog. Muffled banging and shouting reaches you from the valleys below. Up higher in the grey murk, behind the Windamere Hotel, is Observatory Hill, a rather depressing, grubby collection of small temples and flag-bedecked shrines sacred to Shiva devotees and Buddhists, and swarming with monkeys. Here the crowds have a purpose: worship. The drone of prayers being offered up by the monks on Observatory Hill is ceaseless. But down below on Chowrasta everyone is just sitting in the damp air, looking. A few tourists can be seen wandering in and out of the bookshop, the curio shops, the pashmina shops and the cafés, but for the most part the locals are just sitting around the edge of the square, looking. I've sat here and people-watched myself every day since I arrived. Nobody ever bothers you; nobody seems, in this setting at least, to want anything. It's innocent in a way it hardly could be at home. Time is not marked on Chowrasta by minutes but by impressions, by small detonations of sound and colour. Here time stops flying like an arrow and starts to dance.

Amit Chaudhuri also recommends balconies as a place for city-dwellers to spectate, leaning this time on the balustrade. He recommends them in particular for those seeking inner peace. 'What do they see?' he asks of these watchers. There is no answer (in his book, at least). They see whatever is there. Passing through the Gold Coast recently on my way to Brisbane, gazing up at the skyscraper apartment blocks lining the highway like the sides of a canyon, I was astounded to see that on this particular fine Friday morning every balcony in sight was empty. There were forty-storey-high walls of balconies wherever I looked (this being a seaside resort, a holiday mecca, a paradise for leisure-seekers, the embodiment of the relaxed lifestyle, although still, miraculously, 'fast-paced' and 'pulsating', if you believe the brochures), there were great shining slabs of balconies soaring up into the cloudless blue, each one furnished with tables and chairs and usually a pot plant or two, but no people at all. Nobody. Nobody in Coolangatta, Broadbeach, Surfers Paradise or Southport, nobody in Mermaid Beach, Miami or at Burleigh Heads, nobody anywhere had chosen to spectate on their balcony. Nobody was sunbaking. Nobody was even idly reading a newspaper. We don't do it. We don't know how. Are we afraid that somebody will think we're spying on them? Spying is unsavoury. Spying is not looking in the *fainéant* sense – the sense of doing nothing at all. Spying is what children do in adventure books, spying is what the lost souls in Alan Bennett monologues do through the venetians, spying is what the old and chronically bored do to relieve their boredom. Spying is not looking.

In Western countries idly looking is, however, socially acceptable in a rural setting, especially near water – a river, a lake, the sea, anything watery. Or near mountains. Is it a matter of looking at what we all agree is a view? (Bizarrely, on Chowrasta nobody ever looks outwards to where the view should be, the mountain view, which in fine weather is breathtaking beyond all imagining, if the pictures in the brochures are accurate. On Chowrasta everyone looks inwards at the square.)

Views as such, it is alleged, came into being on the 26th of April 1336. Before that date, on which the Italian poet Petrarch climbed Mont Ventoux in Provence simply to look at what could be seen from the top, there's no evidence that anyone – any hermit or cowherd, any pilgrim or traveller – had ever looked out and down on the world just for the poetic feelings that what they saw might arouse in them. Or even at a lake or seascape. They must have, on countless occasions, but since there's no evidence of it, the British art historian Kenneth Clark declared Petrarch to be the first man to climb a mountain for its own sake, and to enjoy the view from the top. Indeed, he declared him to be the first modern man. Nobody has bothered to argue with him.

Writing to a former confessor, Petrarch himself claimed that he'd climbed the highest mountain in that part of France for no other reason than to see what so great an elevation had to offer. He was dazed, he wrote, by the vast sweep of the view spread out before him. He claimed, as no mountain climber had ever claimed (in writing) before him, to have been 'bent on pleasure' and anxious that his enjoyment should be 'unalloyed'. (Leisure in a nutshell, really.) Before Petrarch, it seems, people surveyed the scene from an elevated position for a purpose: on the watch for enemy troops, to search for lost sheep, to keep an eye on what the neighbours were doing. In many parts of the world people also climbed mountains to commune with the gods, as they still do right here on Observatory Hill: a mountain peak seems to offer a view across the threshold between this world and the next. The Greek gods live on top of a mountain, not at the bottom of a lake; Moses climbed Mount Sinai, he didn't have his audience with Jehovah beside the Red Sea. At the top of a mountain you have nothing higher to aspire to, as it were. All you can do is come down. So we have sacred mountains all over the planet, but almost no sacred valleys – secret, but not sacred.

Nowadays, seven hundred years after Petrarch, looking at a view for its own sake is something we all indulge in whenever we get the chance. Planeloads, indeed trainloads of people come here to Darjeeling every single day to look at the view – nothing else, just look at it. The road up from Siliguri is jammed with traffic day and night – buses, vans, taxis and cars full of people coming here to look at the view. At home we even design and build houses specifically to provide what is termed a 'stare-view' from the living room and possibly a bedroom or two, although rarely any other part of the house – a bathroom with a view, for instance, is still considered an amusing eccentricity. When I'm at the weekender, at the desk in the living room, I often write looking at a nicely framed view of forested hills: it provides a sort of counterpoint to the busyness in my head, keeping me on the alert. Despite the fact that, as far as I can see, nothing much ever happens out there – a pair of black cockatoos might swoop past, screeching amicably, a curtain of rain might drift in from the west, obscuring the valley – looking at this vista provides me with a kind of second self without my moving an inch.

In Australia we have lookouts (as we call them) where you not only may, but are indeed encouraged to stand and stare. Local councils often signpost them so that tourists driving by can stop, point their mobile phones at them and drive on inwardly refreshed. What is it, though, that traditionally refreshes us at a lookout?

In a sense, every view offers us a hint of the sublime, surely – a rush of terror while staying safe. Every view contains a dash, however faint, of the epiphanic. Even an ocean view on a calm, sunny day can provoke thoughts of what lurks beneath the waves: on the one hand, nothing at all, unending gloom; on the other hand, death from drowning, death from a lurking stonefish, death from a shark attack, death from a giant squid. Monsters or nothingness: in either case oblivion. Yet here on the beach or the headland we are untouchable. On the edge of an escarpment in the Alps it's much the same thing: staring out into the void we have thoughts of death from cold, or death from a fall, or death from an avalanche, or death from a suicidal leap, or, in the Himalayas, death from a sudden landslide or a pouncing snow leopard (rare but imaginable). Looking, we are two people. This is literally ecstasy: standing outside yourself in a direct sense. This kind of 'double life', as Peter Timms has called it in his musings on views in *Making Nature*, is unlikely in a paddock.

A view can also provide a narrative, which looking across a plain cannot, especially if it's carefully framed, as many of the panoramas offered by our lookouts are. Some even have a touch of theatre in the broadest sense of the word. The first view I can remember ever seeing as a child was at Echo Point in the Blue Mountains west of Sydney: hardly a drop at all by Nepalese or Swiss standards, but by my standards as a six-year-old local spine-tingling. It wasn't just a matter of the sheer cliffs, the certainty of death if you slipped, the hostile bush-covered landscapes empty of life yet at the same time seething with death-dealing animals – well, snakes and spiders, anyway. It was the stories of the first explorers from a century and a half before, the thoughts of convict chain gangs, the questions about how the people on the farms we could make out far below us first settled there, how they got there, where the road was and who had built it. There was a narrative, in other words, to dwell on, as there inevitably is along any coastline as well: of smugglers and pirates (if you've been reading Enid Blyton), shipwrecks, adventure, invasions, arrivals and departures. Again, you don't get that – not really, not quite so dramatically – on the flat. On the flat – out walking in the country, for instance, looking at green folds in the landscape, perhaps at a river – you might get a pleasing prospect or two, but that's not a view. Kevin McCloud, the presenter of *Grand Designs*, is forever declaring any greenish outlook with a tree and an old barn in it 'spectacular', but, living as I do in Tasmania, I am more demanding.

I don't believe that we enjoy views, even commanding views (as they are revealingly called), principally because of the power they endow us with, as some theorists have suggested. Yes, in some cases we might have the illusion of omnipotence: looking out and down (as we do as a rule – rarely up) we see the world in miniature, like a model landscape we can refashion as we wish. In general, though, I think it's subtler than that. I think views are a permitted way of looking because of the added pleasures they afford without inciting us to break rules or behave badly. Staring at the night sky is similar: it both amplifies your sense of who you are and annihilates you in the same instant, it is terrifying and magnificent, familiar and utterly alien. It is perfectly acceptable to stare at it in wonder. Not for long, of course, any more than you can stare at the sea or the view from Mont Ventoux for long before you start to feel empty and want to go home. There's nothing more boring than the infinite. And spelling it with a capital 'I' doesn't make it any more appealing.

Just for the record, I'm unconvinced by Petrarch's elegant protestations about only wanting to see the view from the top of Mont Ventoux for its own sake. In reality, reading his letter to his confessor a little more attentively, I think it's fairly clear that young Francesco was, firstly, heartsick for Italy and desperate for a glimpse of his beloved homeland (not far away to the east, but I doubt you can see it from Mont Ventoux), so he was using his time on top of the mountain to think about the myriad ways in which he'd changed over the ten years since he'd left Bologna – to rehearse his life, in other words, to conceive of it as an unfolding narrative, as we're all apt to do on mountaintops; and he was also, importantly, in the grand tradition of mountain climbers across the globe, from South America to Japan, the Holy Land and Europe, looking on his walk up the mountain as an allegory for drawing closer to Heaven and leaving 'earthly things' behind. His book of choice for his daytrip, after all, was St Augustine's *Confessions*.

There's no Petrarch in the Mayfair library, a cosy room lined with hundreds of books of every kind from bodice-rippers to the *Encyclopaedia Britannica*. That's where I like to take tea sometimes, ensconced in one of the large, comfortable chairs with some unlikely volume plucked from the shelves – something about the old Sikkimese royal court, say, or Joanna Trollope. No Petrarch on the shelves, but there are bits and pieces of him in the reference books. (Does anyone ever take these tomes down and read them?) 'How earnestly we should strive,' he avers in his letter to his confessor from atop Mont Ventoux, 'not to stand on mountaintops, but to trample beneath us those appetites which spring from earthly impulses.' Indeed, towards the end of his letter he assures his confessor that he feels angry with himself for still admiring earthly things when he really ought to have long ago learnt that nothing is 'wonderful' but the soul, which, 'when great itself, finds nothing great outside itself'. Of course, an earnest motive is perfectly compatible with leisure, so long as it essentially still has pleasure at its heart and is freely chosen. He may have been indulging in leisure, but Petrarch wasn't doing almost nothing. Whatever he was doing, he clearly wasn't loafing.

There is one quasi-magical thing you can do with a view that, oddly enough, is very like smoking: hang-gliding. It's one of the things I truly regret never having tried and now never shall. High up near the Rohtang Pass in Himachal Pradesh, at several spots beside the road overlooking a heart-stopping, sheer drop into the valley you've just driven slowly up from, there are groups of young men trying to stop your car and talk you into leaping off the edge into the void with one of them, borne aloft by a brilliantly coloured hang-glider. Vultures gather with a kind of morose hopefulness in small clutches on nearby boulders. It would, I know, have been one of the most euphorically transformative experiences I could ever have had. It would have left peering out over the Jamison Valley from the lookout at Echo Point seeming practically ho-hum. It would have wrenched Echo Point out of the sublime category and made it run of the mill. That is to say, in joyfully jumping out into the view, pinned under a swarthy instructor, for the first time in my life I could have died and not died simultaneously. I would have been doing both something momentous and absolutely nothing at all, and this, I would argue, is leisure at its most refined, its most enlightened.

Doing more something than nothing

One deeply pleasurable way to spend time is in idle conversation, although it's arguably an art that's in decline, what with clocks and the industrial revolution and the common male need to make announcements. I don't mean vapid chitchat at a party with a glass in your hand, your eyes roaming the room for someone more amusing to latch onto – there's nothing fecund about that – but intercourse you can drift with, bob along on like a boat, companionably admiring the prospects opening up on all sides, but at the same time delighting in the glimpses afforded you of something more intimate.

Before the onslaught of social media, Indians had it down to a tee. In West Bengal, where it's hanging on by the skin of its teeth, they perfected a kind of conversation that is doing a bit more something than nothing (but not much) called *adda*. An *addabaj* will join his friends for unhurried conversation about things that matter, usually over tea or coffee, in a way that is quite private, despite taking place in public. So the discussion will be both private and out in the world. The participants do not gather in order to gossip, or to perform for each other as the French did in their salons, or to teach anybody anything, or to buy or sell anything, but to exchange views without fear of reprisal, to learn, to argue, to be actively curious. It's not a competition or a boozy shouting match in a pub. The locals claim it's quint-essentially Bengali, yet many other peoples must have indulged in it in some form or other over the centuries (the Spaniards, the Turks, the Egyptians, the Khmer, the Uzbeks – and surely the Ancient Greeks). Still, I can see what its Bengali aficionados mean: in today's world it's very Indian.

I've only done it once, by the way, at the Indian Coffee House off College Street in Calcutta. In this legendary cauldron of left-wing thought on several floors around a deep atrium, the air was thick with smoke, the coffee abysmal, the waiters surly, the food hardly worth putting in your mouth, but the conversation was electric. Everyone at our table was a revolutionary – middle-class, young, angry, curious, harmless and excellent company. I stayed for hours.

Adda is doomed, or at least fading. Partly this is because a new Lego architecture is taking over in Indian cities, even in Calcutta, even in South Calcutta – you can't lounge around on the front porch anymore, half-inside and half-outside, watching the street-life over a cup of tea for hours on end as you chat and spar: there is no front porch. And partly it's because everyone now in India, from the beggar slumped against the wall with his begging-bowl beside him to the smart young things roaring around town in foreign sports cars, gathers in a virtual space for discussion – or at least to trade snippets of information – not a physical space. Almost everyone's time is for sale nowadays, too – free time is drying up.

The word *adda* apparently comes from a word for birds nesting. Yet nothing could be more profoundly human, surely.

~

Although the light is disappearing and the fog thickening, I think I'll go for a walk – nothing too purposeful, but it won't be 'pure vagrancy', either. I'm really not very good at complete idleness, and the closer it gets to doing nothing, whatever I might theoretically believe, the more fidgety I become. I'm more comfortable veering towards the doing-something end of the scale.

If done properly, of course, whether in the country or the city, walking *can* give us the feeling of doing something and nothing at the same time. In fact, to loaf while walking requires considerable finesse, so it rarely does these days. Still, it's not impossible. As a rule, when we walk, we move decisively away from mistily contemplating the infinite: *pace* Plutarch and the odd itinerant monk, walking is agreeably rooted in the finite here and now. Somewhere or other recently – was it in the Indonesian writer Goenawan Mohamad's essay on trees? – I came across a reference to the Sufic notion of discovering the self-manifestation of the Ineffable while walking in a forest, a glimpse of the Divine behind the seventy thousand veils of light and darkness God hides behind for reasons best known to Himself. For many of us, daytime walking is frequently about trees (in city parks and lightly wooded areas beyond the city limits), I can agree with that, but rarely about communing with anything ineffable lurking in the green half-light of their branches. It's about being in the world – mindfully, but in the world. People toss the word 'spiritual' around to describe their emotions when they see a lot of trees, but trees are not spiritual. Nor are emotions.

All too easily walking can slew sharply towards the downright purposeful: people walk for their health, to get somewhere, to exercise the dog, to be seen, or even to showcase themselves – market themselves, really – as they do in the late afternoon in towns all over Italy or all day in the Tuileries in Paris.

However, it's true that walkers can sometimes have the pleasant illusion of doing virtually nothing, especially in the country. It happens when they feel completely disentangled from the usual 'web of exchanges', as the French philosopher Frédéric Gros puts it, 'no longer reduced to a junction in the network redistributing information, images and goods'. The walker, according to Gros, is free to see that 'these things have only the reality and importance you give them'. I liked the sound of this when I first read it – he goes too far, of course, as French philosophers often do, but the notion is seductive. In fact, I wrote out quite a few of his thoughts on walking at the back of my diary to chew over as I walked. (Not that I've walked much up here in Darjeeling or on the tea estate – the paths are too steep for comfort, the sky too low, the feral dogs too menacing.) Ideally – and is this ever really possible? – Gros thinks that walkers might even occasionally manage to *be* nobody, freeing themselves of history itself. Being nobody is not quite the same thing as doing nothing, but there's a connection, surely. Or would be if you could achieve it. (Needless to say, I've never even come close.) Apart from anything else, to be nobody – absolutely and totally nobody, a blank slate – would call for what Gros terms the 'dissipation of our language' – a tall order anywhere, as I've averred, but especially in India. Not a taciturn people, the Indians, and they're everywhere. The erasure of language can only be approached if you are alone on the edges of what 'absolutely endures' – in a word, of what we once thought of as nature. One of the problems of the way we live now is that, firstly, except in the high fastnesses of the Andes or the Himalayas, nothing much even appears to 'absolutely endure'; and, secondly, we are always in touch with the ephemeral through technology in ways earlier walkers were not. We are ceaselessly bombarded with inconsequential exchanges wherever we go in ways we once were not. The evanescent fills our days, the everlasting is elusive.

If, for the sake of convenience, Petrarch is thought of as the first European to admire a view for the pure pleasure of doing so, we like to think of William Wordsworth and his sister, four and a half centuries later, as the first Europeans to walk in nature for the pure pleasure of it, rather than to get anywhere. Wordsworth, as one historian of walking pithily puts it, took walking out of the garden. Once the countryside became, broadly speaking, safe, this was possible. The Wordsworths weren't doing nothing, but they weren't putting one foot in front of the other in order to arrive anywhere or sell anything, either, let alone conquer or pillage; they were not pedlars or vagabonds, and certainly not footpads. They were intent, in other words, on enjoying *being* in nature, not on traversing it.

Clearly, people had been wandering about the countryside on foot, however unsafe it was, for hundreds of years before the English siblings started *rambling* at the end of the eighteenth century. They may not have rambled often enough for them to need a precise word for it much before the early seventeenth century, but they must have done it. We know some Ancient Greeks did it – sauntered out into the countryside to refresh themselves – because Socrates said that he couldn't think of anything more boring. The countryside, he said, mistaking leisure for self-improvement, had nothing to teach him. Not a rambler, Socrates. Did the Romans ramble? A certain class must have. Surely Virgil rambled. They had slaves and soldiers to do the serious cross-country walking, or running in the case of slaves (which is why they were called *servi currentes*), and, like the Greeks, had a whole culture of strolling about their cities, but did they ramble? I seem to recall a story about Spanish tribesmen in Roman Spain being flabbergasted at the sight of Roman officers out for a country ramble: thinking they were mad, the natives tried to shepherd them back to their camp. You should either sit down and rest, they told them, or get up and fight. As a rule in Roman Spain walking was evidently something you did solely to get from here to there. In Japan Kenkō was 'rambling' (according to the English version of his *Essays in Idleness*) to his heart's delight in the early fourteenth century. There is no bliss to compare, he wrote, with wandering in secluded spots in the countryside, where grass is green and water clear.

Rousseau, the man who first inspired the Wordsworths to set out on their walks, was not in fact a rambler: Rousseau was by his own admission a *promeneur*, not a *randonneur* – a walker, not a rambler. The notion that he was some kind of savage, beyond society, is ludicrous: there were real savages in existence on the planet in the 1770s and 1780s, but few in France and Rousseau wasn't one of them. And Rousseau certainly didn't try to make himself nobody: 'Never did I think so much, exist so vividly, and experience so much,' he wrote, 'never have I been so much myself . . . as in the journeys I have taken alone and on foot.'

Nowadays, by way of contrast, the word 'ramble' occurs in the pages of the *New York Times* about once every two days, I read recently, but this may be connected with the attention now given to dementia – I haven't checked. People have always *roamed* – the Goths roamed Europe, the Vandals roamed across North Africa, highwaymen roamed the highways, and so on; but, unlike rambling, roaming implies being on the lookout for something, quite often something that isn't yours: you may not have a definite plan while roaming, but you could well have an objective. Throughout history, people have often *meandered* as well, with some vague connotation of constantly winding back on themselves like a slowly moving river, but rivers are ultimately going somewhere, however indirectly. *Wandering* in some form or other has gone on since time began, but there's a hint in this word, surely, of not just not knowing where you're headed, but being vaguely lost. *Sauntering* is more about what you do with your legs and torso than whether or not you know where you're going; it's above all about your gait, which will be leisurely with just a touch of the dandyish about it. *Amble* is close to ramble, although, again, ambling is descriptive of gait more than anything else – an unhurried gait, the gait of someone with time on his hands. (Do we speak of a woman 'ambling'? Is 'ambling' quite seemly in a woman? Did Mme Swann 'amble', for instance? Surely she 'strolled', her silken parasol at the ready, escorted by a host of well-dressed gentlemen.) *Strolling* makes you think of leisurely walking (walking for the idle pleasure of it), but not far: you can no doubt take a stroll along a country lane, but are more likely to stroll along city streets or through a city park than through a forest or across a moor. My excursions on foot from the Mayfair to Chowrasta are strolls. No, only rambling seems to cover what the Wordsworths did: it's terribly eighteenth-century, nicely English, performed in safety in what passes in England for nature, rather than an aristocrat's garden or in parklands, and, although no longer simply something the gentry indulged in, is still not the sort of thing peasants might permit themselves.

These days there's even less nature left in England or France in which to become nobody, certainly in Gros' sense of the 'absolutely enduring', than in Rousseau's and the Wordsworths' time, but the English and French think there is, and for them that's the main thing. In other words, there's not much raw left in Europe, everything's been cooked. Shocked by the real thing when they get to Tasmania, where I live, English visitors call what they see 'wilderness'. The French are simply stumped. They typically cast about, try *forêt*, and then give up and call it *le bush*.

Up here in the foothills of the Himalayas there is and there isn't a lot of raw left – it depends a bit on the altitude. Here a different verb entirely holds sway: *trek*. It's not Rousseauesque, it's not Wordsworthian, it's . . . Actually, God alone knows what it is. There were two strapping young women at breakfast the day before yesterday, seriously kitted out for *something*. Their boots were works of art. They certainly weren't dressed for a mere stroll into town. 'Sandakphu,' the one from Melbourne said (the fiercer of the two) when I asked where she and her companion were headed. 'We're doing the Sandakphu trek.'

'Ah,' I said, as I usually do in this sort of situation.

'Five days,' said her companion, piling yoghurt and berries on top of her muesli. She was a sturdy, curly-headed young woman who sounded South African. A nurse? She eyed me up and down. I am not strapping.

'Tents?' I asked.

'No, huts.'

'Ah.'

I felt oddly envious. It would be sublime. Even in the damp, even if the rhododendrons had long ago lost their blooms, even if the glimpses of the Himalayan peaks were few and far between, it would be awe-inspiringly beautiful out there on the ridges beneath the peaks and in the lush valleys, eagles circling overhead, the forests alive with . . .

'Snow leopards – no danger from snow leopards?'

They chortled, but not quite chummily. 'I doubt we'll spot a snow leopard,' said the one from Melbourne (indeed a paramedic). 'That *would* be a treat. A red panda, maybe, or a barking deer.'

'Plenty of birds, though,' said her fellow trekker. 'The foothills are a paradise for birdwatchers. Do you like birds?'

'Quite,' I said. I was eaten up with envy by now. The Sandakphu trek would exalt the spirits, it would induce a kind of rapture, it would be unforgettable. It would be beyond me. I could never do it. It would be the epitome of leisure, despite being at the doing-something end of the walking scale, but I couldn't do it now.

'Jeep to Rimbik, and then we walk.'

If I'd been a prince, I might have ordered a palanquin and gone with them.

∼

Rambling in the city is a different kettle of fish altogether and always has been. Although certain Athenians enjoyed a stroll around the agora, it usually had a purpose: to buttonhole other Athenians and engage in conversation as they walked. In fact, the word 'agora' seems to come from a root meaning 'to converse' while, fascinatingly, in Greek *peripatein* means to walk with overtones of talking as you do so. Why doesn't English have a verb like this? Perhaps 'comport oneself' comes close. Rome was rowdier: Juvenal declared a walk through city streets to be asking for trouble – you could be robbed, knifed, beaten up or 'brained' (my friend Stephen Miller's term) by a falling tile. In his lively recent history of walking around Manhattan (*Walking New York* – no preposition) Stephen has a lot of fun listing famous people who liked and did not like walking through city streets on both sides of the Atlantic: as you'd expect, the English poet Thomas Gray, who coined the phrase 'far from the madding crowd' and is remembered mostly for his elegy written in a churchyard in Stoke Poges, Buckinghamshire, disliked coming to town at all; as did his contemporary across the Channel, Rousseau, and the essayist William Hazlitt.

By way of contrast, Hazlitt's friend Charles Lamb, another essayist of great refinement, loved the bustle and wickedness of London, not caring a fig if he ever saw another mountain in his life; Max Beerbohm, while not admitting to loving the vice and sin of the roistering city, derided the pretentiousness of those who thought walking in the country was somehow nobler and more virtuous than walking in the city; in Paris, Baudelaire famously found city strolls intoxicating (thereby leading Walter Benjamin and his crowd of academic followers way up the garden path, as we shall see, where they loiter, bemused but convinced they're on the track of something, to this day); and Charles Dickens liked nothing better than what he called 'a little amateur vagrancy' in the city. Over in New York, his near-contemporary Walt Whitman found the concentration of wealth and industry, the 'turbulent, fleshy, sensual, eating, drinking and breeding' crowds he encountered in the stinking streets amongst the whores, the thieves and herds of pigs rooting about in ankle-deep filth 'electric' (naturally).

Even if Western cities, at least on the surface, are less menacing, less riotous places than they were in Lamb's or Whitman's day, lounging about the streets of a city, unless undertaken with considerable panache, can still turn too easily into skulking and soliciting. When he was living in New York many years ago, long before we met, my own partner, Peter, mastered the art. He used to go walking in Manhattan in an enviably idle way, combining loitering with what Dickens called walking 'straight on end to a definite goal'. He would set out for the nearest street corner and cross in whichever direction was showing a green WALK sign and then walk on to the next corner. He sometimes roamed around Manhattan for hours in this way, he remembers, usually until he ended up somewhere he found too seedy for comfort, when he would turn heel and get out, having seen things he could never have planned to see. This kind of idle perambulation also appeals to me: it's without any purpose or objective, yet not totally at random – there's a pattern of sorts to it. You can be both engaged and withdrawn at the same time. New York, with its vast grid of straight streets, is no doubt the perfect place to walk in this way. It wouldn't work everywhere. We now live in a town, rather than a city. It's not easy to walk like this in a town because you know it inside out.

Another friend of mine, Richard, a man in his early fifties just back from Madrid, has also mastered the art of walking idly through a cityscape. He not only knows how to saunter, stroll and amble, he's a dab hand at mooching about. I envy him. He's practised it in Cuba, where he spends a lot of time, but he perfected it in Madrid.

Echoing Pooh Bear, I asked him once how he does it. 'I set off on my own for the day,' he said, after contemplating the question for several minutes at his leisure, 'with just a vague idea of where I want to go and which direction to take, but not much more than that. Any arrangement to meet anybody – Steve or somebody, say, in front of the Círculo de Bellas Artes at three o'clock – would spoil it.' Even Steve? I am surprised. Steve is his life companion, Steve is as attuned to Cuban and Spanish rhythms as he is. 'Steve wants to know why we're going in this direction and not that, why we're going down this particular street, why we're not heading for this museum or church or these gardens. Why does he have to know? I don't need to know.' Richard considered some more the question of how he likes to walk, his thoughts clearly drifting back to Madrid. 'To walk idly,' he said, 'means leaving things open-ended but with a few possibilities in mind.' This kind of indeterminacy immediately appealed to me. 'It means giving up definite objectives and just walking and then seeing where you end up.' There's something about Richard's attitude to walking that reminds me of good conversation: you don't know *exactly* what you want to say until you say it. It's in saying it that you find out.

Richard doesn't always walk alone. 'I have this friend in Madrid,' he said, 'who would call around for me in the evening and we'd set off into the night, heading

in no particular direction, but with a few ideas of things
we might enjoy – a favourite tapas bar where we might
stand around for a while, a Gaudí apartment block he
said looked wonderful "sleeping" in the early hours of
the morning, with nobody around . . . It could have
been anything. This is how I most enjoyed spending
time.' Time – yes. Richard is unafraid of time. And
consequently he has managed to come just about as
close to walking while loafing, or loafing while walking,
as it is possible to come. This is the 'mingling of the
errand and the epiphany' that Rebecca Solnit writes
about in her celebrated meditation on walking in the
city, *Wanderlust*. If only I could do what Richard does!
I'm ripe for an epiphany. Do I even have the talent?

Richard's kind of urban roaming is in practice for men
only, particularly after sunset. During the day, while her
husband, Digby, was at the office, Elizabeth, Brookner's
heroine, used to mostly shop and cook, but she did also
walk, she says, presumably around South Kensington,

> although I hardly saw my surroundings, those dull, almost
> handsome streets and squares, where I might encounter
> a neighbour, on the same shopping expedition designed
> to furnish a quiet afternoon . . . there was no pleasure in
> these walks but they were my harmless way of damping
> down any incipient dissatisfaction that I might have felt.

London is uneventful, her life is uneventful. She is 'furnishing' time so it might appear less vacant, less infinite. Unless accompanied by a dog, or obviously shopping, a woman sauntering along a city street like this, completely alone, will be taken, almost anywhere in the world and particularly after dark, to be either soliciting or mad. In a movie I was watching a few weeks ago set in New York and drawing on the life of Diane Arbus, Nicole Kidman says to her husband one night, 'I think I'll go for a walk.' Really? Alone at night? In New York? Unlikely. Virginia Woolf might go for a walk every day alone on the Downs, but the idea of Nicole Kidman going for a walk alone in Manhattan at night arouses our suspicions. Needless to say, she doesn't 'go for a walk' at all – even in a movie as crammed full of improbabilities as this one, we know Nicole is lying. She's going to see Robert Downey Jnr. Now, that makes perfect sense. (If you're wondering what it is about dogs and strolling aimlessly, it's worth remembering that a dog is one of the few animals that enjoy walking idly in the way humans do – taking their time, investigating, sniffing the breeze, simply mucking about. Certain pigs and the odd goat will also be up for it.)

Once Elizabeth's husband has died (it was terribly sudden: a seizure at the office), she does in fact take to walking alone around South Kensington and adjacent parts of London either at night or in the gloom of the early morning. These are the only times there are 'no witnesses' and she can be sure of not being recognised. 'I may have had a genuine physical longing for fresh air,' she writes, 'but what I really wanted was an illusion of liberty, of freedom . . .' Composing a life for herself that has no boundaries, makes no demands on her time, imposes no inescapable duties, is 'easier to contemplate in the dark than in ordinary daylight'. For Elizabeth, newly widowed but provided for, walking becomes 'the main business of the day'. All the same, without a dog, she runs a risk.

My friend Richard's accounts of walking around Madrid remind me that walking with a friend is not the same thing as walking alone. What is the difference?

Walking alone in the mist and drizzle along the Mall Road to Chowrasta, for example, past the wistfully named hotels (Matterhorn, Dolphin, Dreamland, Nirvana) and the stalls selling things I don't want, dodging groups of frisky schoolchildren and tourists from the plains, I can see that my notion of myself as 'a junction in the network redistributing information, images and goods' does indeed fade a little, and, as Gros predicted, I become as much 'nobody' as it's possible to become at my age after a lifetime of saying 'I' to all and sundry every day. Darjeeling is a town, of course, not open countryside, but still, by the time I get to Chowrasta and merge with the crowd of loafers loafing there in the damp, I have

in point of fact turned into a sort of *roving* junction
of impressions, one not patched into any network at
all, with little sense of history (a whiff of the Raj, but
no personal history), on the edge of wordlessness in the
eddies of Bengali and Nepali I've been drifting in and
out of along the way, especially where the roadway cuts
through that patch of forest. Yes, alone I am in a sense
left with my mind's eye fixed only on what is enduring,
not on myself – there's a grain of truth in all that, even
here in town. With a companion, it would be quite
different – with Shubham, for instance, who's actually
got the rest of the day off, he told me while pouring the
tea at breakfast, and would like nothing better than to
show me hidden corners of Darjeeling and practise his
English. ('Would you like to see the Jew?' he asked me
in a stage whisper, offering me more marmalade. 'The
Jew?' 'The Jew. Not bore. They got snow leopard. But
closed on Thursdays.') With Shubham I'd be *somebody*,
definitely somebody. I'd look and talk from a chosen
position in the network of language, culture and desire;
I would have a past, a sense of humour, an awareness
of the rules (and how they might be bent). This would
not be a better way to walk, but indeed a quite different
one. It would not be walking with another as Socrates
did it; it would not be in any way an exercise in self-
improvement (for me, at least). Instead, I would have
a sense of time being spent pleasurably, sociably and

amorally. What Shubham would have, I can't say. I suppose he would experience the eros of language, my English words a kind of arrow to the heart. Who knows?

⌒

Neither kind of walking – around Madrid in Richard's case or around Darjeeling in mine, with or without Shubham – would be *flânerie* in the modern, fashionable sense spawned by the German thinker Walter Benjamin. At least, I don't think so: he means so many things by this one word that it's hard to be sure. Just talking and writing about the *flâneur* is now an industry, the words themselves bought and sold as a commodity right across North America and Western Europe (as anyone who has read Benjamin might have suspected they would be). 'All of us are prostitutes,' one of his aficionadas has written disarmingly, no doubt for a respectable fee, 'selling ourselves to strangers.' I think she needs to meet more prostitutes: to sell yourself is not necessarily to prostitute yourself.

Obviously both Richard and I are *flâneurs* in the common or garden sense of the word – we wander slowly and idly about cities not our own, seeking not knowledge but experience *for its own sake*; we practise 'the ambulatory gaze'; we are part of the crowd as we stroll, yet are detached from it, our eyes (and ears and noses) searching out things it barely notices; we love carrying out our *flânerie* in cities, where the interiors of the buildings we're passing spill out onto pavements. But Benjamin in his *Passagen-Werk* (*The Arcades Project*) forces the word to mean much more. I don't think that, strictly speaking, either Richard or I are ever *flâneurs* in the sense that Benjamin concocted so productively on reading Baudelaire.

In fact, I wonder if anyone really is. How much actual *flânerie* in Benjamin's sense is going on in modern cities? Even along the stretch of Parisian boulevards Benjamin was focused on (between the Church of the Madeleine and the boulevard de Bonne Nouvelle – the northern edge of the second arrondissement, basically) it's debatable: I know the stretch reasonably well, and it's hard to pick out anyone there now who isn't a tourist on a shopping expedition or a swindler from the Balkans. There's not much 'ambiguity' to walking along city pavements nowadays: everyone is either buying or selling or walking the dog. How much *flânerie* in his sense *ever* went on is also doubtful: as far as I can see, his intricate ideas about nineteenth-century strollers, ambiguously subverting what it meant to be part of a crowd (hiding in it, getting in its way), unproductive amongst feverish productivity, neither consuming nor consumed in the midst of rampant consumerism, are drawn not from life but from reading poets of the Second Empire.

We never actually meet one of these *flâneurs* subverting modern capitalism on a real pavement. The idea of them is seductive, but oddly phantasmagorical.

In the early twenty-first century in urban centres we meet people doing a multiplicity of things, consciously and unconsciously, but rarely ambiguously. We don't meet a lot of *flâneurs*. We sit in cafés, often in laneways and arcades, acting as virtual sandwich boards for the businesses whose comestibles we're consuming (as Benjamin in effect predicted all *flâneurs* would end up doing), but we don't stroll. Nowadays our boulevard in Benjamin's sense is the internet. This is where we're most likely to stroll at our leisure, chatting with passers-by as well as merchants, often ambiguously, even under a pseudonym – unless, like Richard and me, we're actual tourists, exploring new places. Even then, it's now eccentric, surely. Overwhelmingly, not just here in India but across the globe, tourists move about in packs with a leader. It's a cheap and practical way to travel, but a group is also, of course, the perfect target for merchants intent on packaging up our time for us and selling it back to us as a managed leisure activity with value-added features.

⌒

One place where we can still loiter, loaf and lounge about with impunity is the seaside. Here languor is licensed and a degree of dalliance expected, although, if we wish, while lying lazily on the sand, we can contemplate others being yet more active – catching waves, swimming out to sea, playing beach volleyball, skateboarding along the esplanade or just horsing around.

Not content with doing nothing on their estates in the country, the English upper classes have been going to the seaside to be idle for almost three hundred years. It all began in Scarborough, apparently, a long-established spa town for the aristocracy, where the first bathing machines were rolled out in 1735 or thereabouts and the pursuit of health began to give way to frivolous pleasure-seeking. Then King George IV took a liking to Brighton, and Queen Victoria to the Isle of Wight and Ramsgate, and before you knew it, with the arrival of the first steam trains the lower classes were frolicking at Blackpool and holiday-making was born. Why were the English the first? Because the sea was never far away, their workers had holidays and, now, trains. When the railway reached Nice, royalty went there, too – even Victoria went to the Riviera – followed by lesser mortals in their millions, often far from modestly dressed.

But wait: didn't the Roman upper classes flock to Baiae on the Bay of Naples two thousand years earlier, to lie about on the sand, snog, and worse, and then dash into the water to disport themselves and cool off? The resort town of Baiae was famous for its sexual diversions by Ovid's time and a hotbed of vice by Seneca's, but the Romans probably didn't just lie around on the beach reading the latest scrolls and feasting on hotdogs with cheese. They did read papyrus scrolls for pleasure and did feast on takeaway sausages on bread with cheese, but not, as far as we know, on the sand while their children bobbed up and down in the waves. It was the English who first came up with the idea of lounging about doing basically nothing on a strip of crushed shell and rock at the edge of the sea, simply for the fun of it, showing a bit of flesh. I've seen Berliners doing nothing, stark naked, in the sun in parks around Berlin, but it's not the same. You can't do nothing in a city park at the same pitch as you can at the beach, on the very edge of nothingness. A lake is never quite the same, either.

Less than a century after Victoria went to Nice, Alberto Moravia set *Agostino* on an Italian beach. (I'm pacing myself with *Agostino* because it's so short. All the same, it's hard to read it slowly because it's so enticing, I'm so beguiled by it – now I've bitten into it, I want to polish off the whole thing on the spot.) Wherever Moravia's beach was, it was hardly a fashionable resort, but it could stand for beaches everywhere, from Scarborough under George II to Waikiki today. On this beach, where Agostino and his mother have come to spend the summer, the thirteen-year-old boy starts to hatch into a man. Becoming a man, he believes, will be the solution to all the turbulence afflicting him. Doesn't every boy think that when puberty strikes?

All Agostino achieves in the course of this short novel is the loss of his childhood innocence about sex. In the company of his new sexually aware young companions, he leaves childhood behind, but fails, of course, to turn into a man. Itself a narrow zone of transition between nature and civilisation, the beach has long been a place of sexual transition as well, at least in societies such as ours where, as my friend Drusilla Modjeska has pointed out, we have no agreed way of marking the turning of boys into men, as they do through ceremony in Papua New Guinea, for example, and any number of other more traditional societies. In fact, she says, we largely refuse to recognise the problem. I think she's right. We all too often initiate boys into manhood through mob violence, warfare and displays of brute appetite.

What has changed since I was Agostino's age is the freedom we had then to simply loll on the sand, oily and almost naked, going nut-brown in the sun. In those days on the other side of the world from Moravia's nameless beach, a decade or two after Agostino first experienced adult lust (feeling the first stirrings of desire for his sexually adventurous mother, hating her for making him desire her, desperate to break through into full manhood), we too were all flocking to the beach to grow up – or, at holiday times, once we'd grown up, to unplug ourselves from daily life and do nothing, looking at nothing (or nothing much). A few of us surfed in an amateurish, exhilarating way when we got too hot, but you didn't have to. You could just look at sand, water, sky and bodies.

Iconic Australian paintings of the beach, such as Ethel Carrick's *Manly Beach – Summer is Here* (1913) or Charles Meere's *Australian Beach Pattern* (1940), not to mention Max Dupain's photographs from the 1930s, show Australian beach-goers lounging, playing, sunbaking, disporting themselves and generally relaxing, either fully clothed or in bathing costumes, on the beach. They are 'titillated' by the sea, as one critic has written, they romp at its edge, they poke a toe into it, they do not 'embrace' it. On Marina Beach in Chennai this is still how the beach is enjoyed, I noticed recently: people talk, promenade, play chasings, fly kites, ride horses, sell snacks to each other and slurp on ice-creams, but almost nobody even wades, let alone dives into the Bay of Bengal. At home in Australia few choose to do even this at the beach anymore. Sometimes on a hot day at the main beach near where I live, there will be groups of teenagers talking or larking about on the steps down to the sand; a few parents with small children paddling in the shallows; one or two boys might be resting on the pontoon before swimming back to shore; and on the rocks towards the point there might be a handful of fishermen trying their luck. But the days of countless bodies sprawled half-asleep in the sun on brightly striped beach-towels have largely gone. Do beach-towels even exist anymore? Do striped deckchairs?

Nowadays to lie baking in the sun, even when covered in sunscreen, seems a kind of half-witted thing to do, I suppose, too risky to really be fun, not unlike bungee-jumping. It was never universally popular, even before sunburn could kill you. Theodor Adorne, in his usual cheerless fashion, called grilling yourself brown in the sun 'merely for the sake of a sun-tan . . . not at all enjoyable . . . very possibly . . . physically unpleasant, and [it] certainly impoverishes the mind'. In any case, few seem to congregate physically to lie around doing almost nothing on the sand anymore: most people now hang about in a virtual world, not in a world of tanning bodies stretched out on towels on the sand by the sea. At that beach near our house on a summer's afternoon there might be a few teenagers texting each other on the lawn near the barbecues, perhaps, a kayaker or two pushing into the water at the southern end where their kayaks are stacked, lots of dog-walkers ambling with their pooches along the esplanade, a pensioner or two parked on a bench chatting, even a few eccentrics playing pétanque, but nobody at all doing nothing. Nowadays everyone's got to appear to be doing *something*.

Apart from all that, who needs a stretch of sand to hone their sexual skills or for dalliance these days? Who needs a beach to flesh out their sexual fantasies? Beaches are for surfing. Surfing is certainly leisure, but it's not a version of doing practically nothing, any more than big-game fishing is. It's not loafing, it's sport.

∾

I saw it. At the very last moment I saw it. I saw the mountain.

Up there somewhere in the sky beyond all the milky nothingness the sun had just risen. I was in the foyer, suitcase beside me, waiting for the driver. Ten minutes to go, then I'd be off.

'So today,' the receptionist says with a perky smile (she must have just come on duty), 'you go to . . . ?'

'Khajuraho.'

'Ah, Khajuraho . . .' she murmurs, trailing off a little huskily. 'I've never been to Khajuraho.' A wistful smile.

'It's not easy to get to from here,' I say. 'It's halfway across the country, isn't it?'

'To be honest,' she goes on, turning to stare at the fog, 'I've never been anywhere much – well, just down to Siliguri a few times, but nowhere else, not even to Calcutta.'

'One day, I'm sure,' I say brightly. She turns back to look at me and smiles wanly. I know what she's thinking: 'No, probably not.' Just past Siliguri is where I'm headed this morning – three hours winding down the mountain to the plain, through Siliguri, which is all traffic chaos and squalor and billboards for private clinics, and then on to Bagdogra to the provincial airport serving this tiny pocket of West Bengal, squeezed between Nepal and Bhutan in the Himalayan foothills. I'm not looking forward to it.

Suddenly the sun comes out. With eight minutes left in Darjeeling, the sun comes out. It's like a supernatural apparition – an abrupt manifestation of the sun god (whatever his name is) with his three eyes and four hands. Or four eyes and three hands. (I've stayed in a hotel named after him, but can't for the life of me think what he's called . . .) SURYA! It's like Surya bursting through the clouds in his chariot. It's divine.

I've got seven minutes.

'I'm going to run up the steps to the lookout and see if I can see Kanchenjunga,' I say.

'Today is not visible,' she says, wan to the last.

'All the same,' I say, striding to the door, 'I'm going to run up and see. Back in a minute.'

Up I go, past the hotel's Shiva shrine to the roadway, the sun still shining in a startled sort of way. I run across the street and around to the Mall Road on the other side.

And there it is, Kanchenjunga, gleaming glacially, vast, unearthly, stretched out along the northern horizon high above the Matterhorn Hotel. All around me Indians are gathering, staring in awe and taking photographs of themselves in front of it. Now, *this* is everlasting, *this* is godlike. I feel my very being die away before it. Then it is gone. It's not the minutes, though, it's the experience, it's being alive to something, it's remembering.

I run back down into the swirling moistness to the foyer. The driver is there. We career off into the grey and green and head downhill, dodging between the coaches and trucks and darting pedestrians, the cripples and goats and schoolchildren running for the bus. Someone has just driven off the road and disappeared into the fog-filled valley below. A real estate advertisement on a hoarding beside the gap he's made in the safety barrier announces: SOMETHING HAS JUST GOT A WHOLE LOT BETTER. We nudge our way through the throng of onlookers and continue on down. Down to the plain, the sun and the heat.

Khajuraho. I'm quite in the mood for erotic temple carvings. Darjeeling has been memorable, but a little too other-worldly for my frame of mind – moist, certainly, but hardly steamy.

I'm starting to think that Monsieur Gustave's remark to his Lobby Boy, Zero, about there being no point in doing anything because 'it's all over in the blink of an eye . . . and the next thing you know, rigor mortis sets in' is just the sort of thing a busy man would say. Monsieur Gustave, who was as busy as a hornet in spring, should have loafed more. Then, perhaps, life would not have appeared to have flown by before he knew it. The less you do, after all, the more slowly time passes. Goethe once commented that idleness made time 'unbearably long' while 'doing things' shortened it. Yes, rigor mortis will still eventually set in, it's true, but it doesn't have to be in the blink of an eye. Zero seems to have come to the same conclusion. The last we see of him, as an old man, he's lounging happily in a spa bath in the bowels of his very own Grand Budapest Hotel.

Needless to say, you have to be happy to be idle (not idle to be happy). I doubt that Monsieur Gustave was ever a truly happy man.

Nesting and grooming

We must build a house, but afterwards we must nest in it.

Josef Pieper, *Leisure: The Basis of Culture* (1952)

Nesting

We've just spent a surprisingly satisfying morning throwing things out – nesting, in other words. It's been nesting of the purest kind, so we're both feeling marvellously refreshed: no visits to the hardware store, no browsing for anything online, no repainting, recarpeting or replanting, no commerce of any kind, just good, old-fashioned tossing-out.

It doesn't look like nesting, I know. All those empty cupboards and drawers don't look like the result of nesting. When a dog or a cat starts nesting, it goes around collecting precisely what we've been throwing out, making a nice, soft pile of all those old shirts and blankets and moth-eaten sweaters in a sheltered spot to nestle its newborns in – not so much the books and files and battered suitcases, although sometimes even they might come in handy.

Yet nesting is definitely what we've been doing, I can feel it deep inside me. The arrival of offspring may be the last thing on our minds, but, speaking for myself, I'm feeling what I can only call 'broody' this morning. Yes, *something* is quietly hatching inside me. I might even say that in my own fashion I'm helping to ready our nest for new life. As soon as I'd finished breakfast I started filling bags and bins with things I'd outlived. I showed no mercy. Now and again at the end of our working day or week or year, and often at the end of our working lives, this is what we humans do: we return to what I might call life's grand simplicities. Kenkō, I remember, wrote in his *Essays in Idleness* (which aren't really essays or much concerned with idleness) about the need to attend before anything else to food, clothing and our 'dwelling' – this, he said, was the chief business of man. As an afterthought he added healing and music. At Khajuraho in northern India, where I have just spent a few days, the astounding bas-reliefs on the temples remind us that, for Hindus, at the heart of our present notion of self are what we might call new life in all its forms and the things we do at home – including sex. It's not so different from Kenkō's approach, except in emphasis. Across the centuries people everywhere love to nest.

We've thrown out so much outworn *stuff* this morning between us that we're tempted to make a special trip to the tip to get rid of it all. A trip to the tip can be seriously revitalising – I always come back elated, eager to throw more things out. From sunrise to sunset our local tip is aswarm with householders lining up to sling things into the skips and the state-of-the-art garbage hopper: on weekends the caravan of trucks, trailers and cars crammed with clutter seems endless. The mood is always upbeat, determined. Everyone is actively nesting.

There's no ragpicking at our tip: it's managed decomposition, a solemn symphony of putrefaction, almost picturesque. In fact, it's not even a tip anymore: it's a Waste Management Facility. You can sense everyone thinking to themselves as they ditch the rosebush cuttings, the mattresses, the boxes of yellowing news-papers, the old toasters and juicers, and the various contraptions that seemed like a good idea at the time (the Maximulcher, for instance, that's bigger than I am but couldn't mulch a blade of grass): my new garden (or kitchen or bedroom or shed) starts *now*, I can't wait to get back to it.

The choice of ways to nest when we're master of our own time is wide: from darning socks to pruning fruit trees, from playing the piano to brushing the dog, from polishing the car to polishing the silver and experiment-ing with meringues. And there's sex, too, of course, alone or with a friend. So long as these activities are freely chosen for the pleasures they offer (more or less, at some level) and not merely for their usefulness, they are leisure. For some of us – my friend Isabel, for instance – even ironing is a pleasure, an exercise in focused thought, a freely offered, soothing act of kindness to herself and others. Truly.

Given that so much hard physical labour is involved in some of these activities – and never mind building stone walls: try cooking rendang for six without servants sometime – in what sense are they pleasurable? Full-time idlers of the Tom Hodgkinson variety show no interest in nesting, I notice, aside from sex of a kind he rather off-puttingly calls 'messy, drunken, bawdy, lazy'. Most of us do, though. But why do I feel my leisure time is well spent making a chocolate cake or cleaning out the back room, while you, say, clearly blossom, look positively vivified, as you head off into the back garden after lunch in grubby overalls, with no list of things to get done, exactly like my friend Richard in Madrid, leaving the afternoon open-ended, although with a few enjoyable possibilities in mind? You come back inside hours later tired out, yet supremely satisfied with the way you've spent your free time; you come back into the house profoundly at home with yourself. Is this perhaps the key – being at home with yourself? A living-out of a special kind of intimacy with yourself impossible in the wider world? Since decomposition so often follows hard on the heels of a good day's nesting, I wonder, too, if 'composition' might be another word to capture one of nesting's core pleasures: in cooking soup or knitting socks or repainting the front door . . . what colour shall I call it? Deep burgundy? Perhaps I am recomposing myself in a way that gladdens the heart for the days to come.

Be that as it may, few novelists seem to compose anything about this kind of satisfaction, presumably because it's too subdued for most storytellers, too undramatic. My much-loved Russian novelist Ivan

Turgenev used to finish his novels, or even finish off his characters, at the point where home-making threatened. You want to *set up house* with me and . . . have *breakfast* and . . . even *children* with me? Then sorry, but it's typhoid fever for you, Anna Andreyevna or whatever your name is – or at the very least a nunnery. Courtship fascinated Turgenev, but not marriage, not domesticity. Leo Tolstoy, on the other hand, was notoriously in favour of it. In *War and Peace* what could be more dispiriting than the picture he draws at the novel's end of happy families leading almost boundlessly boring lives centred on the nursery? It's about as interesting as a plate of couscous. Dickens had a penchant for domesticity, too, but didn't try to incorporate it too boldly into a novel.

For some artists it's been a different matter. In fact, it's been suggested that it was none other than the Dutch painter Johannes Vermeer who invented domesticity with his luminous depictions of daily life at home in seventeenth-century Delft: a milkmaid pouring milk, a young woman playing the virginal, a painter painting, a gathering around a table with food and drink on it – in a word, people busy with food and household chores, people eating, being artistic and flirting inside at home. Early last century Pierre Bonnard famously painted domesticity, as did Édouard Vuillard at about the same time. 'I paint people in their homes,' Vuillard said with admirable simplicity, although he didn't always.

Exquisite composition was what these artists excelled at. They were both called intimists – depicting domestic intimacy was what they most notably did, 'speaking' (as André Gide put it) in a low tone, suitable for confidences. When you think of their paintings, you think of smallness, gentleness, richly rather than brightly coloured interiors (as well as some gardens – in Delft there had been no gardens), you think of a brooding quality (often) and the muted presence of family members (sweeping, sitting at table, taking a bath). You think of tablecloths and tea things and beloved dogs. You are suffused as you contemplate their work with a kind of tenderness.

Few would think of claiming that either Bonnard or Vuillard was a great painter – neither was a thinker, neither was a Picasso or even a Matisse – yet they both captured with feeling and an insouciant wit something so ordinary that virtually no other modern painter has even bothered to try to depict it: what it felt like to be simply at home.

Has David Hockney tried, perhaps? On reflection, I think he might have here and there. He is surely the most accomplished of today's intimists. Few Australians, though, have taken the trouble. When it comes to leisure, Australians overwhelmingly choose to paint their compatriots in social rather than domestic situations: at the beach, playing sport, in bars and parks and on the street, even at the theatre or dancing, but almost never just being themselves at home, quietly nesting. (Just sitting is hardly nesting.) Grace Cossington Smith has some vividly coloured paintings of suburban interiors, but there's rarely anybody in them. Her sock-knitter is knitting for the war effort.

When we think of Pierre Bonnard, on the other hand, we think first, surely, of several of his famous evocations of serene domesticity. In *The Dining Room in the Country* (1913), for instance, one of his most loved canvases, showing the dining room of his house at Vernonnet with the door open onto the garden, much of the nesting has already happened – the fruit has been picked and laid out on plates on the table, the red poppies have been arranged in a vase – but his wife, Marthe, can still be seen at the window, bent busying herself outside in the light-filled garden, while two cats are sitting on chairs, eyeing each other, ready for mischief. The basic elements in the scenario of domesticity are there to savour: food, gardens and, unobtrusively, once we know who's at the window, a tender sexual attachment. When he painted this room twelve years later in *The Dining Room*, for all the changes in tonality and the dog's snout poking up above the rim of the blue table, the same elements are still present: food on the table, flowers in a vase, and this time a reflection of Marthe outside in the garden. It's true that nobody is caught in the act of cooking here, or sweeping or picking fruit, but it's clear that this is what somebody's been doing. The monotonous and easy tasks of everyday life (in those days almost exclusively performed by women, of course) are in progress, as they always are in middle-class homes. Something is happening: the figures are not sitters.

In our nests we do many things, not all of them nesting and some more by choice than others. Traditionally, women have never been truly free at home unless born to privilege – hence the need to indulge in a little idle needlework now and again, even if you were a princess, to show that free and privileged is precisely what you were. These days in the suburbs practically all of us, men and women, do have times when we can choose how we might nest. There are myriad cleaning and tidying jobs we perform every day to keep ourselves presentable and in running order (unless we're rich), and there are always a few decorating and do-it-yourself tasks to potter at around the house as well (loftily dismissed by Adorno as 'pseudo-activity' – he was not the home handyman's friend), but nesting's sturdiest roots are in the business of food, gardening and sexual intimacy. A nest is scarcely a nest without at least one of them. They resonate with each other, needless to say, in both life and art, although if the only garden we can enjoy at home is a row of succulents on a window ledge, and if our food is consumed above all to keep us

healthy, and if sex for us is no longer reliably more fun
than watching the football on the telly, then we may not
fully appreciate how interconnected gardens, food and
sex once were.

ↄ

Eating obviously shares a lot with sex: as the Indian food
critic and cultural historian Pushpesh Pant has put it,
eating, like sex, consumes all five senses and is marked
by the same cycle of anticipation, ecstatic absorption
and satiation. Even if you think 'ecstatic' is going a bit
far, you can see what he means. Hindu cosmogony's
Primal Nipple springs to mind. Actually, nipples in
general spring to mind.

Eating, some have claimed, has several advantages
over sex. 'In the first place,' my friend Chandrahas said
to me recently (and he's well placed to judge), 'food is
a sensual realm where the gulf between your imagination and reality is much smaller than it is in . . .' 'Yes,' I
said, and cast my mind back. He paused to help himself
to something piping hot and creamy. 'And secondly, with
food, looks are irrelevant.' 'Yes,' I said again, not much
cheered – well, I'm not much of a foodie. 'And thirdly,
there's much less mess to clean up afterwards.' That, as
we know, depends on who's been doing the cooking.

As with most things dilettantish and amateur in
modern life, the pleasures of preparing a meal and

inviting others to your table have been well and truly appropriated by professionals. This is partly true of gardening as well, but gardening has been so radically eclipsed by cooking and eating in recent years, its place in the public arena now so shrunken, that it's hard to judge to what extent the professionals have taken over. Their triumph in the very heart of the suburban home is particularly galling because, since at least Victorian times, this space has been the preserve of the non-professional occupations. To put it more bluntly, it has belonged to women. In modern usage the very words 'amateur' and 'dilettante' are derogatory. As a flagrant dilettante in virtually every department of life, most at home writing or reading at the kitchen table, I naturally take exception to this – fruitlessly, but I do.

In the kitchen, for instance, it's now impossible to just muck about concocting things for fun without images of Nigella Lawson, Jamie Oliver or (even more alarmingly) Poh popping into your head: faultlessly attired, a smile on their lip-balmed lips, gleaming pots and pans in readiness on their gleaming stoves, all the ingredients they need right there on the bench, even the pomegranate molasses, even the Nepalese goat's cheese, even the sour fish sauce from the island of Flores, each and every one of them correctly measured out in gleaming little containers. Nothing burns, nothing so much as overcooks. Everything is perfect. Nigella,

Jamie and Poh all smile and gleam. In fact, Poh is often in such uncontrollably high spirits, she appears to be having a seizure. Consequently, the wind is taken out of your sails before you can so much as find a clean saucepan to fry the onions in. You – and don't you forget it – are an amateur. You can buy their books and DVDs, you can follow one of them up the Mekong or watch another cook up a storm in some Sardinian peasant's hut, you can even watch master chefs fight it out like feudal knights in fantasy arenas (we were addicted to *Iron Chef* at our place for years – to the chefs' impassive expressions, to the subtle cruelty of the judges; each week it was a brutal medieval tournament), but you yourself remain an amateur. You always will be an amateur. You learn nothing from the celebrities – and don't expect to. Who watches the celebrities to learn anything? Cooking is now show business, not adult education; it's Broadway, Hollywood and Bollywood combined, and you haven't got so much as a bit part in any of it. Cooking, it slowly dawns on you, is now not so much something you do as a commodity: they sell, you buy. You might serve up a super little *borchtch à l'orange* (with a dollop of smetana, God forbid it should be local sour cream) next time your golf-club friends come to dinner, but you're still basically buying. You might even do what Walter Benjamin predicted you'd do (I can see his point about this): you might act as a sandwich board for a celebrity

116

chef. 'The lamb rump with vanilla-braised chicory and sorrel pesto? Rick Stein. No, wait a minute – it's from the new Ottolenghi. Have you got it? Believe me, it's one of his must-haves. Gay? I have no idea.' (The last bit is of commercial use in certain company only.) Meanwhile, they are selling. Jamie Oliver, for instance, sells very well indeed: according to one website, he is now worth about half a billion dollars, on a par with Madonna. He's ahead of the pack by only a whisker.

Yes, it's true, we are all free to whip up a salad and throw a few snags on the barbie any time we like, invite a friend or two around to share the grub and tuck in. In theory. In practice it should be . . . Well, a brand of barbecue your friends will recognise as superior. With a roasting hood and a triple brass-ring wok burner and heavy-duty lockable castors and stainless-steel knobs and . . . In other words, these days, an old wire grid balanced on bricks over a fire doesn't quite cut the mustard. This isn't having friends around for a beer and a couple of burnt sausages, this is outdoor entertaining, this is your version of show business – amateur show business in your case – *South Pacific*, as it were, staged as a fundraiser for the local girl guides. To paraphrase the almost unreadable Walter Benjamin, for whom I really don't have much time at all, in fact virtually none, cooking is now either a chore or another bit of nesting that's been turned into a commodity. Open your wallet and pay up. That is how capitalism works.

Eating is another matter. The principal threat to eating as a form of leisure comes from its ordinariness and our lack of choice about whether we eat or don't eat. We have to do it every day whether we want to or not. Most people do want to, but not everybody: Will Self, for instance, in one of his grumpier moods, once observed that food was just shit waiting to happen. It can be more than that, but I know precisely what he meant: sometimes it's quite nice, but, like Christmas, food almost never lives up to its promise. It sustains and is then excreted. A slice of stilton on a crisp, buttered biscuit is almost convulsively delicious, I agree, but who can afford to eat stilton every afternoon? (I like it at five.) Maggie Beer ice-cream with rhubarb cooked in orange juice is unarguably heaven; a finely judged affogato ambrosial (if you can linger over it); caviar on fresh bread with creamy butter (as we had it in Russia once upon a time) exquisite; a tart green apple on a warm afternoon delectable; my own fish soup at the very least delicious, even if I do say so myself . . . But I digress: in my experience, *pace* Pushpesh Pant, food is rarely memorable, let alone ecstatically absorbing or satiating. In any case, it's been clinically proven that most people, blindfolded, can't tell a slice of eye fillet in a Dijon mustard sauce (with just a hint of lemon – don't overdo it) from a bowl of cornflakes.

Many people are reconnected with their cultural roots when they eat, some (to judge by their overwrought behaviour on programs such as *Food Safari*) ecstatically. Reconnecting you with your roots is exactly what leisure at its best does – I know that, it just doesn't work for me. My roots are in chop and three veg, with Chinese on my birthday. I don't feel ecstatic about it. If you genuinely want a sensual extravaganza that galvanises your cultural roots, how about ballroom dancing, and more specifically the tango, with someone you're crazy about every inch of? In my heyday I would stay awake all night after only two hours of ballroom dancing, every sense not just aroused but at fever pitch. This has never happened with sushi.

Amateur gardening, once as fashionable as food has become, is in steep decline. Over recent decades suburbia, which is where it happens, has changed radically.

Not that you'd think so if you were standing where I am, looking out through the back windows onto the garden behind the house. At the bottom of the garden, where the back fence is almost entirely hidden by a nectarine tree and a Japanese maple, Peter is up a ladder, awkwardly pruning the nectarine in the late-afternoon sunshine.

At first glance this scene looks like the very essence of age-old nesting – even primordial nesting, going right back to Adam and his fruit trees in the Garden of Eden. And while our back garden is hardly bigger than a tennis court, it *is* in a way (I think to myself, mistily, enjoying the sun) our little Eden, our stab at paradise in the suburbs. How right it feels to watch Peter playing Adam. Who was it once said that gardening was the 'purest of human pleasures' since God was the first gardener? Francis Bacon, I think. (No, not that one, the other one.)

But that's nonsense. Thousands of years ago in the wilderness between the Tigris and the Euphrates the locals might well have pictured Paradise as a garden full of fruit trees and greenery for food, but today in Battery Point, Tasmania, our backyard is not Paradise: it is a decorative space in a range of reds, blues and purples to maintain at our leisure and to grow rhubarb, lemons and a few apples in (the birds get most of the nectarines). We maintain it so that we can do precisely what I am doing now: look at it with calm satisfaction through the sunroom window. Its beauty is very Japanese, lying in its evanescence, its propensity to rot, in the way it hovers between order and chaos. The front garden, which is a narrow profusion of native ferns to the right and camellias with a single yellow rosebush to the left, exists to be looked at with pleasure from the street. Around the corner a neighbour has persimmons in the front garden, but this is an eccentricity on his part: front gardens are for show, not for fruitfulness; nobody grows carrots or broad beans in the front garden. (Except Italians.)

We don't even grow carrots or broad beans in our back garden anymore. A few years ago we did. Once upon a time, during the heyday of gardening in Australia, we also grew broccoli, potatoes, lettuces and various kinds of tomatoes. We had peach trees and apricot trees, a passionfruit vine and grapes. We once had chooks. We were fecund. At some point after the war, with the gradual disappearance of woodpiles, sheds and outdoor toilets, the suburban backyard turned into a place where a man might spend his leisure hours building up garden beds to plant vegetables in and tending to his pride and joy: the lawn. Mowing it, weeding it, feeding it. Every man who had a house (there was always something slightly pansy about men in flats) had a lawn. A backyard was inconceivable without a lawn. It might have had a border of annuals for popping into vases around the house (zinnias were a favourite), but at its heart was a lawn. The woman of the house was more likely to be seen weeding the front garden, clipping the hedge on a weekday morning, perhaps, to show the world that she had no need to go out to work, or in winter pruning the roses lined up in gay abundance along the front fence. There are still such gardeners to be seen, but rarely emulated, on the one remaining television program devoted to this now barely remembered kind of gardening. Nowadays I can walk for hours around the streets of my own suburb, even on a fine Saturday afternoon, and see nobody – no one at all, not a single denizen of Battery Point, apart from the couple across the road, who are artistic – actually gardening. Out the back they will doubtless have decks and entertainment areas, a tree or two, a row of shrubs, and once a month someone from a gardening service might come to keep it all neat and tidy. Professionally. Instead of television programs about gardening, as once we had, we now have television programs about garden makeovers, installing garden furniture and building barbecue areas. Why?

It seems to be partly because, with our increased prosperity, we have found ways to keep the garden looking a picture without having to toil in it. Leisure should never be about toil you haven't chosen to undertake for the pleasure it gives you – and gardening in the old-fashioned sense was always close to being a chore: with half a suburban block given over to a garden in one form or another by the 1960s, you could easily find yourself spending all your spare time working in it, planting, weeding, harvesting, feeding, watering, raking and replenishing. Paradoxically, as Peter himself has remarked, all the labour-saving devices (as they're thought of) gardeners are now tempted to use actually make gardening more of a chore, not less: the whirring brushcutters, the whining hedge-trimmers, the roaring motor-mowers, the mulchers and leaf blowers turn gardening into a dangerous, noisy trial. In addition, with women in increasing numbers working full-time, there are now fewer hands to do the work in the garden. And finally, clinchingly, the fruits of our labours in the garden, whether freely enjoyed or seen as a burden, can these days be so inexpensively and speedily bought. The choice is dazzling in even the most down-at-heel suburb or remote country town, the supply uninterrupted, effortless. You need a pomegranate for the salad you're making? Satsuma plums for your dessert? Creamy potatoes? A vintage tomato? Celery? Turnips? Swedes? Blueberries? Granny Smith apples? Whatever you want, however exotic, however out of season, you can have it now. It may taste bland, but you can have it *now*. Peter up a ladder lopping the nectarine tree is out of step with the times.

But in his case it's leisure at its purest. In leisure at its best, like Jehovah, we look upon our work and find it good. Far from being a chore, for Peter it is more like a quietly pleasurable way to negotiate a response, as a city-dweller, to his love of the wilderness, of nature, of what is still untouched in the world. It's his defence against the city he must live in. In his case, it is indeed (oddly enough, given the century we're living in and all we know) primordial. It is never merely useful nor merely an entertainment. He is composing. In the garden he is more Debussy than Mozart. He is knowing who he is at a profound level.

It is completely out of kilter with the times. If we're of a mind to be a bit wabi-sabi about things (as many people are at present, and speaking of Debussy) – that's to say, neat but not too neat, revelling in impermanence and deferred fulfilment – we can do it more comfortably indoors. 'Deferred fulfilment', you'll say, sounds vaguely erotic. It is.

ↄ

As a form of nesting, sex is not quite so easily taken over by commercial interests and sold back to us for profit as cooking and eating and gardening are. (Sex as business or entertainment is a different matter, obviously.)

Whatever its disadvantages, good sex is a superb way of being at home with yourself – of enhancing your intimacy with yourself (never mind anyone else). It's easy, too, now that we have private, comfortable bedrooms and many men are less anxious about their own virility. We don't talk or write about it much – we talk and write about adultery, we chat about our sexual desires and fetishes online with 'friends' and 'contacts', the discussion itself an erotic performance of sorts, we watch unstable people having sex in dramatic situations on television and at the cinema – but leisurely, forgettable sex at home in the bedroom seems too unremarkable for us to bother commenting on.

A few painters have captured it. An awareness of sex as a fine way to be at home with yourself is something that I believe Bonnard and Hockney share, for instance, improbable as that may sound. Sexually they certainly make an odd couple: the uxorious Bonnard on the one hand, who spent practically his whole life intimately attached to the woman he loved, both as wife and lover, and on the other David Hockney, a bohemian who has had a lifetime of sexual intimacies with men he sometimes lived with and sometimes did not. Yet both are intimists, each of them captures a similar sexual *knowingness*, a moment of sexual apprehension, in the depiction of both nudes and clothed subjects in domestic settings, the sort of moment passed over in some more unambiguously erotic paintings by celebrated modern artists: think of those famous Bonnard images of women bathing and dressing, of indolent nudes and naked couples, of unmade beds and messy dressing-rooms – amazingly matter-of-fact, as they should be at home, as much a part of the way things are as afternoon tea. Pleasure is either idly anticipated or lightly remembered here, as it is in any number of Hockney paintings and sketches.

To take one well-known example: in *Domestic Scene, Los Angeles*, from the early sixties, one man, lightly clad, appears to be washing the back of another young man who is taking a shower; the setting is almost homely, with an armchair, a vase of flowers and even a telephone in the room where the shower-stall is. It doesn't depict anything overtly sexual, yet the pale-buttocked nakedness, as in *Boy About to Take a Shower* (1964) and several other paintings of naked men at home, is distinctly *après* something very sexual indeed. The half-naked youth lying face-down on a single bed (another vase of flowers, a lamp, the glimpse of greenery beyond the French windows) in *The Room Tarzana* (1967) could be satiated or he could be waiting to be satiated – he's certainly wide awake and a little on edge. Whoever he is (probably Peter Schlesinger, his great love at the time), he's not a nude: he's a man in a middle-class bedroom thinking about sex. I find the single bed quite provocative, as I do his white socks. Indeed, I find these naked figures much sexier in general than the swimming-pool nudes Hockney is so famous for: there's a coldness, an uneasy emptiness, to those paintings, for all the sunshine and bright colours, that negate desire.

I wonder if the hazy Hinduism floating about in the balmy air in Los Angeles where Hockney was painting in the sixties had any effect on the easy integration of sexual pleasure into the patterns of domestic leisure in his work. Hinduism (since my balmy evenings in Khajuraho are still firmly in my mind's eye) strikes me as being the religious mind-set most open to the notion of sex as a good way to know yourself inside out and upside down – to enjoy being human, really, when it all boils down to it.

In Khajuraho, which is quite a small town bang in the middle of the North Indian Plain, I liked nothing more at sunset than to sit in the bazaar gazing westwards at its famous domed temples, black against the apricot sky, remembering what I had seen earlier in the day. Westerners flock to Khajuraho to see the twenty or so richly carved temples – there's nothing quite like them left on the face of the planet, a whole airport has been built in the middle of nowhere just so that Westerners can jet in, tour the temples and jet right on out again. It's the temples' gently erotic carvings they're most anxious to see, but the striking thing about the frank depiction of carnal play here is that it appears as just another aspect of daily life: in astounding detail, robust medieval men and women (mostly heavily built, thick-legged) are shown potting, farming, making music, bathing, dressing for the dance, putting on make-up, kissing, and, naturally enough, copulating in ways I doubt even St Paul's debauched Corinthians had thought of. There's nothing else to do here, really, except gaze at the temple carvings – or at least not officially.

I do understand that indulging carnal lusts for the sheer pleasure of it may not be the ideal way to hasten your passage across the threshold towards heightened consciousness. To put it more bluntly, sex-for-fun may hinder the attainment of Enlightenment, especially from an austere, priestly perspective, although, intriguingly, I noticed that many a threshold between profane and sacred spaces in Khajuraho is decorated with a carving of an embracing couple. On the other hand, as the bawdier, far less ascetic Indians who actually built the temples knew, there's nothing better than good sex to put you in touch with all the things that have made you what you are: your needs, your playfulness, your foolishness (lots of foolishness), your kindnesses and greediness, and the things you've learnt over a lifetime about burrowing into somebody's . . . I nearly said 'soul', but let's say 'innermost being'. Whatever the Brahmins might have said over the centuries or social mores might still dictate, at an everyday level the Hindu religion has traditionally accommodated sexual rapture in a way the desert religions do not. For Hindus, after all, desire is the reason that the universe exists in the first place, the reason that there is frenzied twoness all over the place straining for ecstatic oneness. Saints may warn against indulging it, but in India poets and peasants are in no hurry to return to primal cosmic oneness. Hinduism aims as high as any spiritual system, but is realistic.

Most Christians and Muslims, try as they might, can't quite overcome the feeling that sex is *of itself* degrading in some way to somebody – cheapening, demeaning, even shameful – any kind of sex, whether you invite it or not. Even Kenkō, the Buddhist monk whose ramblings I so much admire, a man usually finely attuned to human frailties, cautioned against lewdness and even trying to live with a woman – much better to visit occasionally as a kind of friendly nod to one's fundamental humanity, he said. Living with impermanence when you think there's something better is a challenge: should you just lie back and delight in the impermanent or should you try to rise above it?

Some more modern Buddhists might well enjoy a much more relaxed attitude to sexual pleasure, but Gautama Buddha himself, the Blessed One, took a dour line. Although he called the way between the unworthy, harmful pleasures of the senses and unworthy, harmful self-mortification the Middle Way, he came down hard on the craving for sensual pleasure. Even in the Middle, it seems, you must give up delighting in desire for the impermanent. In his first sermon, for instance, delivered to his first five followers in the Deer Park outside today's Varanasi (often called Benares), he made it quite clear, in his rather intransigent and some might say self-regarding fashion, that suffering will end only when we forsake this craving for the impermanent, which takes us ceaselessly back to being born. Only then can we hope for Enlightenment. Only then can we glimpse the path to *no more becoming.*

In the end, like St Paul half a millennium later, his attitude to sex seems to come down to a preference for abstention, but if you have to have it, at least don't have it with somebody else's wife. Was kissing permitted? I don't mean the kind of Continental fiddle-faddle we all indulge in these days on meeting anybody at all, practically the postman, but kissing on the mouth, kissing in the mouth. I can't get any consensus on this. Kissing on the mouth is an utterly fundamental thing for humans to do: the appetite for somebody else's mouth – the 'nectar' of their kiss – is eros incarnate, pursued not for nourishment (as our first sucking is), not to make children, but for the pleasure of what it is.

On his way from the place where he achieved Buddhahood at the foot of the Bodhi tree to the Deer Park outside Varanasi (pilgrims can fly there direct from Bangkok these days as well as from all over India), this Nepali prince met an ascetic called Upaka who was eager to know whose doctrine the serenely handsome young traveller professed. 'I am all-wise,' the young man replied a trifle off-puttingly, 'detached from all things. I have cast off everything. I have obtained emancipation by the destruction of desire. I have no teacher, no one is equal to me, in the world of men and of gods no being is like me, I am the Holy one, I am the highest teacher, I have extinguished all passion . . .' and so on and so forth for several more minutes. Eventually he summed up his position: 'I have attained the extinction of sensual desire, the lust for life, false views and ignorance. I have overcome all states of sinfulness. I have conquered myself.' A bit taken aback, as you would be, Upaka hurried off. The Buddha trudged on towards Varanasi to expound, for the first time in the history of the world, the Truth. And 'ten thousand world systems quaked and quaked again and shook, and an immeasurable, mighty radiance burst forth, surpassing even the effulgence of the gods'.

To me, this is all deeply unnatural – in fact, it's virtually a perversion of our humanity in the name of an abstraction. In practice, despite their belief in the impermanence of earthly lusts, I don't suppose ordinary Buddhists deny themselves the pleasures and agonies of desire for what is impermanent any more than anyone else does – Genji in *The Tale of Genji*, for all his piety, denied himself absolutely nothing, his appetite for sex was gargantuan, while today the entire population of Bhutan appears devoted to guiltless sexual cavorting. All the same, in my experience, all things considered, Hindus with their pleasure-loving hearts are much less self-important than Buddhists (and Sikhs and

Muslims and Christians), much more suburban and much more fun.

Why this official hostility on the part of the world's religions to something so pleasurable and universal? Some level of self-discipline is in order, clearly, desire being by its very nature unfulfilling and therefore likely to get out of hand, but in the desert religions sex in particular is not just controlled but saturated with anxiety and guilt – it is 'morose, furtive and masturbatory', as one Western expert on Hindu sexual practices has termed it.

It all comes down, surely, to how the different cultures urge this self-control. In Islam self-control seems to be a practical social behaviour rather than a path to oneness with a primal Self, whereas in Christianity and Buddhism it is of spiritual benefit. When Paul (whose ideas about the uses of sexual pleasure were severely limited) told the Corinthians that it was better for the unmarried and for widows to marry than to burn with desire, he prefaced his advice by saying 'if you can't control yourself'. In other words, unless you control your lusts, the Devil can get up to all sorts of mischief with you (especially in Corinth, by all reports) and you can control these lusts or passions or desires best by marrying. An intimate relationship with God is difficult if you are consumed by bodily desires.

Now, late in life, I'm beginning to think that it's Hinduism's approach to sex in daily life that makes the most sense, Hinduism that understands best that religious practice at some level is play. The theological intricacies hold little attraction for me, but Hindu ideas about sex strike me as eminently practical – or at least they were until the Muslims and Christians got to work on them. Release from the cycle of rebirth? Yes, please, but not quite yet.

My guide to the temple complexes around Khajuraho on my first morning there was an amiable, impeccably attired middle-aged man who, as far as I could tell, was happily indifferent to all religions. Neverthe-less, he seemed to take great pleasure in chatting to me about India's main religions and Indian history as we wandered from temple to temple in the heat. The carvings, he said, symbolically highlight the four goals of life considered necessary and proper in Hinduism: observing your community's social and religious codes (*dharma*), sensual pleasure (*kama*), providing materially for your family (*artha*) and the eventual release from the cycle of reincarnation (*moksha*). The point about *kama* or carnal longing at the time these carvings were made, well before the Muslims or Christians had arrived in India to spoil things, is that for Indians, both men and women, it was seen not as something to rush to rise above, but as a normal part of being human – indeed, a duty. The tricky bit, the guide agreed peaceably, was (and is) to make sure *kama* doesn't crowd out the other three goals. In any well-lived life, sexual desire should unfurl like the fan of a peacock's tail and give delight. In Indian love poetry, for instance, as well as Hindu art across the centuries, not only do lovers and wives pine for what was and what is out of reach, but the gods and goddesses themselves pine and come together in sexual ecstasy. Imagine Jesus or Jehovah doing what Radha and Krishna do with such passion and finesse, imagine a Christian saint firing a lotus-tipped arrow at lovers from a bow made from a string of bees, yet the god Kamadeva does.

It's true: to keep your eye on all four goals at once as you go through life, you have to exercise a degree of self-control – not simply in order not to 'burn with desire', as St Paul expressed it, but also in order to be human in a good way. Looking about me as I sat dreaming beside the bazaar in the heat of the evening, I wasn't at all sure that the young men of Khajuraho had all appreciated this need for a balanced mix. As night fell every day, across from the entrance to the temple enclosure, you could feel an erotic skittishness hatching amongst the young men astride their motorbikes and lounging in groups by the side of the road, a sort of jittery fixation on sexual opportunity. These were St Paul's 'unmarried'. And they were burning. Their thoughts were like yo-yos: down, up, down, up, look-at-me, look-at-me. A truck might drive slowly past with a garish, illuminated god on the back, loudspeakers blasting wild music into the sky, young devotees dancing feverishly on the roadway behind it, but I felt no release from anything here, no surge towards supreme Enlightenment. In fact, I felt an uncontrolled convulsiveness. And when the truck had passed, the youths in the warm shadows in the empty bazaar would still be there, watching, chiacking, laughing, calling out. But at that age, on the street, I expect you do. And then you grow up and bit by bit find a better balance, a more intricate way of being human, at least for the time being, at home.

~

Is taking a bath a form of nesting? Barely, it seems to me, but yes, by a whisker.

I've never quite understood the attraction of the bath. Bathing is another matter entirely – when you bathe there are things to do: jump about, swim on your back, hold your friends' heads under the water. While I don't do it as a rule, I can see why you might. The pleasures of the bath, however, remain a mystery. Why of your own free will would you choose to lie in a coffin-shaped contraption full of cooling, grubby water with your head at an awkward angle? People do, though. Now and again, if I'm staying in a nice hotel, I will look at the line-up of de luxe shampoos and unguents and *après bain* dusting powders in the bathroom and feel practically obliged to take a bath. Will I? Won't I? Eventually I run one, delighting in the rush of ozone, wait for it to cool a bit or try to make it hotter (it's never just right), clamber in, look about and within seconds find myself wondering what to do next. Taking a bath is unfailingly a disappointment. Apart from anything else, lying alone in a pool of your own grime seems such an unnatural thing to do for pleasure.

The most refreshing way to clean yourself, if that's your main aim, is surely to take a shower — or, in Indonesia, to sluice yourself all over with cool water from a *mandi*, soap up and then pour a few more scoops of it over yourself. Slosh a scoopful in your face. Then slosh another scoopful over your head. You feel reborn. Then there's the Japanese, who have come up with a unique way to take a bath: first they rinse themselves clean, then they lower themselves into a hot bath to soak and sometimes talk to other bathers, then they get out, soap themselves and rinse off again, and then they climb back into the tank or tub to soak one last time. Or at least some Japanese do this some of the time. It's a big improvement on lying in a tepid pool of your own filth, but it's time-consuming.

As it happens, however, I live with a passionate bath enthusiast: from his point of view, the *sine qua non* of a well-balanced day is a bath at the end of it. No rubber ducky for him or even a loofah. He does like to sip at a small single malt, though, as he lies there under his bubbles listening to something faintly astringent on the Bang & Olufsen. I dare say that for him taking a bath is the perfect way to do nothing and something at the same time, at home, cocooned in the innermost room in the house. As far as he's concerned, it's a very particular blend of restorative nesting and self-pampering. I suspect he's in the majority.

Grooming

Taking a bath, I would maintain, shades into grooming, which is not quite the same thing as nesting because it's not necessarily done at home. Even if it's not done at home, grooming is less fun if it's anonymous – less plea-surable, in other words, at a grand hotel (I mean a *really* grand hotel, not the somewhat down-at-heel Grand Budapest, where I suspect it is always a delight) than at a smaller, more intimate establishment.

There's nothing more pleasurable than a spot of grooming after a morning's (or week's or year's) hunting and gathering, but there's a shift, I think, in the nature of the pleasure it affords in the direction of the more broadly animal. Does this account for the whiff of guilt that sometimes accompanies it? Not always but sometimes, surely: it's a move away from activities responsible for the survival of the species towards lying about like a cat in the sun, lazily licking itself.

At the practical level there's the visit to the hairdresser's to be shampooed and smartened up – an animal pleasure of sorts, if you surrender to it utterly, inhaling deeply and revelling in the application of *product*. It's often the highlight of my week – but then I'm the sort of person who feels pleasantly stirred by the prospect of a visit to the podiatrist, however brief. It's not intoxicating, I don't feel disproportionately aroused, but after ten minutes in a podiatrist's firm hands I feel I know what it is to be a puppy being stroked. (Buying new shoes is a related thrill: it has nothing to do with shopping, it's all about grooming. The smell alone of a shoe shop spells sensual abandon.) Facials, body-waxing and other skin treatments are certainly forms of grooming, but constitute a definite move away from revival after the hunt towards out-and-out self-indulgence.

We've come up with a wonderful word in English to capture this love of spoiling ourselves or surrendering to being spoilt, giving in to the temptation to indulge ourselves excessively for the pure pleasure it bestows on our bodies (and also, we assure ourselves nervously these days, our minds): pampering. It's an old word, originally meaning to overstuff yourself with food, but these days pampering can connote something much daintier, even if at root it still hints at giving free rein to appetites that in the course of daily life are best curbed or dampened down: the urge to be touched in intimate places, to be stroked, to be fed delicacies, to make the body more attractive, to take your ease in ways that could be seen as self-indulgent.

I'm always struck when I travel by how much flagrant pampering is on offer. It's not just in resort towns in South-East Asia, say, where bodily delights are what people are principally there for (not the temples), or in up-market hotels in capital cities all over the globe, where everyone colludes in pretending that busy people need to 'relax' (often in the establishment's watery, and usually steamy, lower depths). A hotel I stayed in not long ago in country New South Wales, for example, claims to offer a 'unique' selection of escapist delights to complement the sophisticated lifestyle of its guests, by which it seems to mean massages or sitting around in a spa pool or sauna – pretty much what hotels from Sydney to Siem Reap and Stockholm offer those at a loose end with plenty of money.

Now, I heartily approve of escapism, but, having tasted these escapist delights over many years in the bowels of a variety of hotels around the world, I have to report that, while it's nice to be massaged, and sometimes very nice indeed (especially in Kerala), it doesn't rejuvenate you, restore you or make you feel anything very much except sleepy – not really, not for more than twenty minutes. It doesn't tone your muscles, loosen your joints or alleviate twinges. A massage is a sensual indulgence (especially, as I say, in Kerala). It is being intimately touched by a stranger (or, in Cambodia, two strangers). You're pampering yourself. A sauna, as I know from living in Helsinki for a while, might well clean out the pores, but that's not why anyone has one. You have one for precisely the same reasons kids go to the local swimming pool (swimming not being one of them). And there's nothing wrong with that, either – occasionally.

Almost everything about the most popular self-pampering activities is flagrantly juvenile, when you think about it: from setting sail on a Caribbean cruise to lolling around in spa tubs, from being massaged with oils and lotions to staring into space surrounded by scented candles. A retreat into childhood? It's practically a return to the womb. And there's nothing wrong with that, either – in moderation.

Whenever I think of the claims made for massages and facials, for sitting in saunas, Turkish baths and bubbling spa pools, as well as for lying in a candlelit hush, drifting off on dreams of your own sandalwood-scented loveliness, Rabelais' green sauce comes instantly to mind. In *Gargantua and Pantagruel,* one of literature's most boisterously comic novels, Pantagruel's companion Panurge is talking up the benefits of the 'lovely green sauce' he makes from corn before it seeds:

. . . it enlivens your brain, gladdens your animal spirits, delights your sight, whets your appetite, flatters your taste-buds, steels your heart, tickles your palate, clarifies your complexion, tones up your muscles, tempers the blood, lightens the diaphragm, freshens up the liver, unbungs the spleen, comforts the kidneys, settles the bladder, limbers up the spondyls, voids the ureters, dilates the spermatic vessels, tightens up the genital sinews, purges the bladder, swells the genitals, retracts the foreskin, hardens the glans and erects the member; it improves the bell and makes you break wind, fart, let off, defecate, urinate, sneeze, hiccup, cough, gob, spew, yawn, dribble snot, breathe deep, breathe in, breathe out, snore, sweat, and get your gimlet up, together with hundreds of other extraordinary benefits.

Sure it does. And I'm Queen Marie of Romania. But I wouldn't mind trying some all the same.

Play

Maturity means to have rediscovered the seriousness one had as a child at play.

Friedrich Nietzsche, *Beyond Good and Evil* (1886)

. . . it is characteristic of play that one plays without reason and there must be no reason for it. Play is its own good reason.

Lin Yutang, *The Importance of Living* (1937)

Now at last it's time to play. It's literally showtime.
Having hunted and eaten and then loafed about at our leisure, doing more or less nothing; having then looked to our nest, composing ourselves anew and taking pleasure in being our everyday selves in it (spruced up a bit from time to time to help us look and feel our best); we're ready now to play. Your idea of play may not be mine, but all of us, whether enjoying a game of bridge or squash with our friends, singing in a choir, collecting Chinese celadon, surfing or skiing or worshipping a deity, are rooting ourselves deeply in our culture. (Which reminds me that across the globe the quintessential sport, according to several esteemed cultural theorists with Germanic surnames, the purest expression of unadulterated play in all its forms, is illicit sex. But I'm getting ahead of myself here.)

Culture *is* playing. Is that *all* it is? High mass in St Peter's, Pushkin's poetry, paintball, Plato's *Symposium*, the slanderous drumming contests of the Eskimos, Monopoly (how I loved Monopoly as a child – or perhaps it was London and money I loved), a game of marbles, Mozart, Monet, the *Mahabharata*, *The Book of Mormon* (as well as the *Book of Mormon*), Madonna and Maori tattoos – all play? Maybe, but what about Frank Gehry's Guggenheim, Genesis, learning German, Quinkan rock art, the Dome of the Rock, corroborees, shopping at David Jones, the *New York Review of Books*,

Christmas with the family, and the corrida? All of them 'playing'? I'm beginning to think so, yes – the lot. (And I'm not alone.)

Not *only* playing, obviously – nobody is suggesting that the Roman Catholic Church, for instance, is nothing more than a game of Ring a Ring o'Roses writ large: whatever weight you choose to give to its performative extravaganzas, it's above all the Roman empire finally falling apart on a street near you. Nobody thinks that when you go off to your yoga or French conversation class, all you're doing is mucking about, filling in time. Even a puppy is not *merely* playing chasings. No, no, the original 'raw' has clearly been 'cooked' over the years (the centuries, the millennia), often overcooked, sometimes burnt to a cinder – yet all culture does arguably come out of raw play. It's our concept of play that may need to be broadened, not our concept of culture.

Is civilisation itself all play as well? No, of course not – at least, I don't think so. The dividing line can be hard to distinguish: washing machines, street lighting, stilton and the rule of law are clearly aspects of civilisation in its various meanings, even if they have cultural ramifications, but parliament, the justice system, democracy itself?

What I'm suggesting is that playing is not *part* of culture, but *is* culture. And it came well before civilisation. The many manifestations of play are what we mean by 'culture'.

Which leaves me wondering whether dogs are cultured. I seem to have cornered myself into saying that they are. No creature plays more purely, more un-self-consciously than a dog, and dogs have been playing since long before civilisation sprouted on the planet. Monkeys and some birds also play, but dogs tick all the boxes. Our dog's effortless understanding of the three main kinds of play will be on display this afternoon when we take her to the beach with her friend, the puggle Twombly: firstly, there will be *competition* (racing for the ball, swimming out for the stick, a vigorous game of tug of war with the screaming child's beach hat); secondly, there will be the theatre of *re-creation* or imitation (killing the hat, hunting the cormorant, chasing Mr Georgopoulos's skittish whippet into the grasses behind the beach, closely followed by Mr Georgopoulos); and, thirdly, there'll be a spot of *romping* – just tearing about, cavorting, frolicking, sniffing, slobbering, falling over with a yelp and occasionally barking – being dogs, in other words. Crucially, it will be voluntary: if they don't want to do it, they won't. There will be skill involved at times, there will be daring and performance, a sense of a playground with boundaries, and pleasure verging on joy. And both our dogs will know, the instant they leap from the car, that the next half an hour is time out from ordinary life at home and won't last long. Every dog also knows that play is best when you're rested and well fed.

When it comes to grasping what play is all about, we seem hardly to have moved on since the first wolves gambolled – or only in the details. In *The Himalaya Club*, for instance, John Lang's account of his stay in a regimental cantonment in Umballah north of Delhi in the 1850s, he claims that the 'principal pastime' was cards and billiards, the players wreathed in cigar smoke, although now and again 'pic-nic [*sic*] and excursion parties are got up, and once or twice a month private theatricals are resorted to'. While smoking and sipping 'some sort of liquid', quite a few of the men also read. Up in the hill station of Mussoorie, in addition to whist and billiards, there were regular balls to focus the attention, and quite a bit of leisurely shopping, especially for fabrics and women's clothes. The slaughter of all sorts of birds and animals was a popular occupation amongst the menfolk for the pure pleasure of killing things. And there were affairs, of course. People eloped with people and never came back, leading in the more sensational cases to actions in Her Majesty's Supreme Court in Calcutta.

Loafing is fun and nesting is deeply satisfying, but playing is leisure at its finest. If freely chosen for the pleasure it gives, it's leisure at its most refined, good living unsurpassed. The joyousness of good play approaches rapture. In a sense, as any worshipper in any temple or mosque or Christian church knows, as does any virtuoso performer on any instrument or any creator of something of great beauty, there is no Good to be sought beyond it. In good play, we touch the very quick of our humanity.

Sadly, good play – transcendent frivolity – is increasingly beyond the reach of most of us until we're too old (too blind, too wheezy, too arthritic, too sluggish, too muddled, too disinclined to go out) to do it with ease. Instead, we might glimpse others doing it on television, although even then rarely: virtually all the play we see on television is competition between professionals (in other words, we're watching highly trained men and women at work); while the kind of play that I've called 're-creation' is something we only come across nowadays in occasional news items or in movies (singing, painting and photography, for instance, or reading, shopping, stamp-collecting, travelling, mountaineering, concert-going, dining out, learning Italian, going to church, chatting with friends and dallying away from home). We *can* do these things – we *can* find time to read books, take a cruise, eat out with friends, go to a movie, spend a week or two in Thailand and so on – but surprisingly few of us do, given our wealth and access to information. We talk about it and watch others do it. As for romping, even the word is out of fashion. Who capers and cavorts these days? Nobody. We have a lot to learn from dogs.

In a world of over seven billion people, group leisure activities are increasingly discouraged by the ruling elites as a threat to public order. Instead of taking pleasure in doing things collectively, we're encouraged now to pay to watch others do things in small groups (at the theatre, on the playing field): it is a 'society of the spectacle', as the French theorist Guy Debord has called it. Sydney has its Gay and Lesbian Mardi Gras, it's true, Berlin its Love Parade, Rio de Janeiro its Carnaval, half the planet football finals, everywhere a New Year's Eve bash, and Allahabad its Kumbh Mela attracting thirty million pilgrims or more *on a single day*, but these are exceptions. The Romans feared the effects of the bacchic rituals on their young men and the Christian establishment did all it could for centuries to clamp down on public festivities of any kind, but in a modern megalopolis of ten million, twenty million, thirty million inhabitants or more, mass festivities really do threaten public order. At the moment some ten per cent of the world's population lives in a city of more than ten million. Collective joy is a public menace.

Competitive play

In *Homo Ludens,* his classic masterpiece, originally published in 1938, about culture as play, Johan Huizinga tells the story of the Shah of Persia who, on a visit to England, was asked (presumably by someone at the very top of the social ladder) if he'd like to go to the races. He declined the invitation because, he said, quite reasonably, he already knew that some horses galloped faster than others. Well, exactly – I couldn't have put the case for never going to the races better myself. (Or to the football or the cricket.) And what was it the broadcaster Phillip Adams once said about football? They should give both teams a ball and then they wouldn't have to fight over it. While half the country secretly agrees with him, I'm sure, to say so is like questioning the sacredness of Anzac Day.

What the Shah of Persia was overlooking, though, and Phillip Adams and I turn a blind eye to, is the fact that going to the races is not about – or only partly about – finding out which horses gallop faster than which, any more than going to the football or cricket is simply about finding out which team will win. It's a failure or refusal to grasp the nature of the rapture (it goes beyond mere excitement) most of our fellow human beings experience while competing or watching others compete. It also shows a disregard for the pleasures of re-enactment. A bonobo monkey has no problem with it, nor does a crow, let alone a chihuahua, but his Imperial Highness did when faced with Ascot.

Winning is not just fun (for many of us, at least) but an exciting part of being human. Men in particular, for hormonal as well as cultural reasons, have a will to win: that's what testosterone is for. Winning is manly and they're men. In warfare, financial speculation and the majority of competitive sports, not to mention violent crime, men shine. Yes, these days both women and men play football, wrestle and box, but football, wrestling and boxing are overwhelmingly male sports. Men want to triumph, defeat, kill and annihilate others, if not on an actual battlefield or in a criminal gang, then on a court or sports field. Our strategies are a cunning hunter's. The grip of such contests on human consciousness is ancient, visceral, evolutionarily vital. It's man and beast, it's war in miniature. Frankly, it leaves me cold.

Horseracing might have left him cold, but I'll bet the King of Kings played the game of kings – after all, he was both Persian and a monarch. One-on-one games of skill such as chess have widespread appeal across the globe. It seems natural to enjoy a spot of tussling and jousting with your fellow man.

Even more popular are games for three, four and more. Some games for two such as Scrabble, checkers and cribbage can accommodate many more players, so that, as well as the game, you get society. Birds, pygmy marmosets, baboons and dogs all love to play with others, as did Her Majesty's Regiments of Foot in India, Lang tells me, as do most people. For some reason I've never much hankered after society, even as a child (especially as a child), but I recognise that most people are enlivened by it. I played Snakes and Ladders once or twice on a rainy afternoon with other boys and girls, I seem to recall, as well as Snap and Happy Families – but who with? I can't now imagine. My cousins at Christmas, perhaps? You would think, then, that I might have been attracted, as millions are, to playing solitary games – jigsaw puzzles, cryptic crosswords, patience, solitaire – pitting my wits against unseen adversaries or chance, but I seem to be missing some basic drive not just to win but to resolve things.

The craze amongst many older Australians for meeting up each week with friends to play mahjong, say, or bridge, has left me untouched. On that tea plantation outside Darjeeling of an early evening, after work finished on the hillside and in the factory, you could usually hear the sounds of bingo numbers being called far, far away below us in the valley where it was already almost dark: 'Fifty-five – snakes alive. Forty-two – Winnie-the-Pooh . . .' As I listened, I felt nothing – just mildly amused at the reach of empire. The rite of gathering regularly to play bingo is as alien to me as clog-dancing.

For whatever reason (only-child syndrome, testos-terone deficiency) I am simply not curious to find out who will win *anything*. According to Huizinga, to what he calls the 'archaic mind' the question of winning or losing was actually more important than being right or wrong. I'm not an egalitarian, but in my moral universe winning and losing just aren't very important.

I've tried to show an interest. I remember, years ago, when I was in my mid-thirties and single, being invited to play poker one Sunday afternoon with six or seven friends from the theatre company I was working with – a motley crew, not all of them kindred spirits, but all talkative, open-minded and up for a good time together. This wasn't *The Sting* or *The Cincinnati Kid*, nobody was armed, there was no Paul Newman or Steve McQueen amongst us that afternoon, although either would have been welcome. In fact, only a couple of us had ever played poker before, as I remember, the rest of us making a show of learning the rules. What we were really gathered in the Bondi flat to do was to frolic with friends – gossip, flirt, tell stories, feel part of the gang – romp together without moving an inch, as it were, not to compete or win. The game was almost beside the point.

All the same, however feeble my drive to win, from an early age I did know modelling when I saw it – re-enactment or re-creation, if you like, what Huizinga calls representation. That must be why I did enjoy Monopoly whenever I got the chance to play it. I loved its strong appeal to the baser instincts, naturally, its snobbery, its genteel viciousness and the piles of brightly coloured cash. But over and above all that there was the allure of the model city, the *play* at living somewhere else, somewhere important, at being a man with money and property but no moral scruples, courting danger, taking risks, being the plaything of chance (as we all are) but at the same time called upon to make decisions, as my father was, with serious consequences . . . until the game ended and we all turned back into our everyday selves again. No wonder half the world still plays Monopoly.

Some kinds of physical competition seem to be between you and nature (or God, if you prefer, or perhaps some lesser demiurge or divinity, depending on your point of view) rather than between you and other people: skiing, for instance, or killing fish – 'angling' as it's called more politely. Killing whatever nature puts in your path will generally do to pass the time. John Lang, for instance, on his rambles around Mussoorie in the Himalayan foothills, shot anything showing signs of life for the sheer sport of it: tigers, deer, birds – he was never without his gun. 'In the course of two hours,' he writes of one encounter with black partridges near his tent, 'I brought down no less than seven brace.' His servant took another five birds. It was as if he was sparring with some spirit of the wild, keeping meticulous score. Is this not why hunters traditionally boast? They've won.

Killing fish, however, is a favourite leisure activity whenever humans have time on their hands near water. It can seem practically refined. Game fishing, though, beloved of wealthy fishermen on powerful cruisers on the high seas, is an unspeakably cruel pastime, on a par with crucifixion drives and bear-baiting, although it can take a gentler, less openly competitive form. We usually come back to town from the shack early on a Sunday morning, and, crossing the causeway near Hobart airport, I always notice the men – there might be one or two women in peaked caps, but it's mostly men and boys – lined up with their fishing rods, doing battle in an almost decorous fashion with chance or kismet or perhaps just a fish. They're angling. Intriguingly, angling, I read recently, is connected to Anglicanism: forbidden to hunt, yet still keen to kill something when they were at a loose end, Anglican clergymen fished. The aura of high-minded contemplation still clings to this form of slaughter. Adam Nicolson, Vita Sackville-West's grandson, a very superior kind of fisherman, as you can imagine, who lives at Sissinghurst and has no need to compete with anybody (being who he is, he's already 'won'), once told me that for him fishing is a 'heightened form of being there'. His mother-in-law told him he only said that because the Eucharist meant nothing to him anymore. I'm sure she was on to something. Still, the Eucharist doesn't mean all that much to me, either, but I've never felt inclined to kill things instead. Of course, fish don't have proper faces, so most of us feel less guilty about putting them to death than we might about bears or antelope. And anglers do often cook and eat what they catch or share the catch with friends, as their ancestors did from necessity. Be that as it may, however ancient the practice being mimicked is when men hunt for the sheer pleasure it gives them, celebrating your deep human roots by killing a creature that poses no threat to you seems primitive to me, more primitive than golf, which is similarly mindful and absorbing to a yogic degree, but kills nothing. It's striking how similar anglers and golfers sound when they start explaining to you why they like doing what they do (which is almost nothing, but not quite, and moderately skilful). None of the fishermen or golfers I know feel completely comfortable loafing. I prefer it, I must admit. For some reason, I feel no guilt at all.

$\backsim$

Golf is not just 'being there', though, in a 'heightened' way, like partaking of the Eucharist, it's also a sport: physical skills requiring stamina are being tested competitively according to agreed rules. Sport is combat turned into leisure. (It is also leisure turned into business, but is not alone in that: as I've observed, most leisure activities have been turned into businesses.) Seeing who can hit a ball into a hole with the least number of strokes falls short of being a culturally fertile occupation. Nevertheless, as a form of sport, it's harmless enough. The Dutch have been hitting balls at targets since at least the thirteenth century. It's tiddlywinks for grown-ups, really – your better class of grown-ups, needless to say, not the sort of people who are drawn to cage-fighting. Who could object to anyone playing a round of golf?

When it comes to vigorously hitting balls, tennis is another competitive game nobody could object to. Tennis, too, is played overwhelmingly by educated people from the right side of the tracks. In a piece in the *Wall Street Journal* reflecting on why he plays tennis, my friend Stephen Miller (always quotable, whatever he writes about) makes sure we note that the group of friends he plays with three or four times a week include the CEO of a corporation, a doctor, three lawyers, an economist, an architect and two heads of nonprofit organisations. It's what I'd have expected. Forklift truck drivers no doubt do play tennis, but not reliably.

Stephen is eager to convince us, as many sportsmen are, that he plays in order to 'become well-tempered', rather like essayist Joseph Addison, who engaged in shadow-boxing and exercising with a dumbbell every morning when in town, and riding a horse when in the country, in order to promote a well-tempered mind.

In this century we'd be more inclined to talk in terms of the beneficial effects of exercise on neurotransmitters or cognitive functioning, but, with his deep knowledge of eighteenth-century English literature, Stephen puts it more elegantly: through 'frequent and violent agitation of the body', he assures us, quoting Samuel Johnson, much happiness is gained and misery escaped. In short, the pleasure of the game for him lies not in winning, but in what he calls 'whacking'. He thinks it's doing him good, both mentally and physically. He thinks it makes him 'whole'. Maybe it does. Who knows? More profoundly, from my point of view, he also says right at the end of the essay that for him 'playing tennis is traveling to a world made simple. When I'm playing, I'm not thinking about myself or my family or what I am writing or the state of the world.' Another friend of mine says precisely the same thing about dressage.

Now we're getting somewhere. It goes without saying that there are benefits to the body and the mind from play. For that matter there are benefits to the body from singing in a choir, but that's not why anyone does it. But *as a leisure pastime* tennis is played for pleasure: pleasure in being engaged in something intensely absorbing that is separate from ordinary life. With its special playground, its rigorous rules and its promotion of social grouping, tennis is perfect. 'Ping-pong for giants', as it's called in the British sitcom *Peep Show*, tennis may well be, but there's nothing wrong with that. It's not leisure when played by Serena Williams or Novak Djokovic, obviously, it's business – big business. But when Stephen plays, despite his eagerness to assure himself and others that it's healthy (Søren Kierkegaard, Saul Bellow and the Italian monk Antonio Scaino da Salò are all recruited to the cause), basically he plays for pleasure. He really likes it.

Of course, tennis, like golf, is harmless. When I pass golf-links or a tennis court, I feel at peace with what I see. Some other forms of competitive play, however, such as football, are far from harmless. The degree of harm depends, as I see it, on what sort of football it is – where it's played, by whom, for what purpose. Cricket purports to offer the dramatic spectacle of a batsman and a bowler locked in a dangerous duel for supremacy in the middle of a vast arena: a ritual entertainment for the spectators, the tense and sometimes rapturous restaging of ancient clan feuding for the participants. It's so boring to watch, as a friend of mine from a cricketing family said to me not long ago, that it's almost like being dead. Its champions might claim that it uniquely combines a team sport with the spectacle of two men pitted against each other until one is defeated, but, having been both dead and forced to play cricket, I know precisely what my friend means. Football, though, is never boring – on occasion, as a spectacle, it is almost sublime, as warfare can be. (And Australians love both with a passion.) But, like warfare, its close cousin, its hold over humanity in recent times is not wholly benign. Worse still, billions of people think football matters. Or am I just parroting here a rather moth-eaten neo-Marxist cliché? Well, it's certainly a neo-Marxist cliché, but I'm not parroting it: I'm convinced it's true.

Originally, before the industrial revolution, football was no doubt a real game, one of many popular forms of play with strict rules for men and boys: skilful, convivial, often violent, of no particular material use – quintessential leisure. In small towns and suburban backyards across the globe, you can still see football being played as it was in various forms for centuries in Europe. As Terry Eagleton observed in an article in the *Guardian* years ago, you have to admit that football blends individual talent and 'selfless teamwork', thereby 'solving a problem over which sociologists have long agonised'. As show business, this sort of balancing of the will to emerge a hero and the need to cooperate with your teammates is thrilling. 'Blind loyalty,' he wrote, 'and internecine rivalry gratify some of our most powerful evolutionary instincts.'

And then something happened: industry arrived. A little later, around the middle of the nineteenth century, both employers and workers agreed, each for their own reasons, that the hours men and women worked should be limited. From the employers' point of view, leisure time promised a more productive, longer-lived workforce, and from the workers' perspective the chance for a bit of fun in their lives before they died prematurely of disease and overwork. As a result, Saturday afternoons were freed up for leisure activities, Sundays being out of the question.

It's worth noting at this point that in many Western countries, as well as Japan, at all levels of society, we're currently edging back again towards living lives totally consumed by work, seven days a week. Not in Italy, obviously, but everywhere else, people are *busy*, and if they're not busy, they're busy trying to convince themselves and other people that they're busy. We're falling over ourselves to sow and reap and gather in barns, with disdain for any lilies of the field we come across. The little time that now remains 'free' we're increasingly inclined to pay to have others manage for us – at the cost to us of working harder. Tourism is an obvious example of this tendency, while at the more culturally barren end of the scale, beyond even yoga selling narcissism as the timeless spiritual wisdom of the East, we have the gym, where, incredibly, hundreds of millions of us choose to fill our free time with what Rebecca Solnit in *Wanderlust* has called 'everyday acts of the farm . . . reprised as empty gestures': pumping, lifting, pulling, straining. The most perverse of these activities is surely the treadmill: on a treadmill you're paying to walk or run.

The powers that be (or, if you prefer, our political masters, the ruling class, the power elite – take your pick) have never felt comfortable with the idea of the hoi polloi having time in which to do whatever they like. They might start rioting. It's a view shared by a number of headmasters I've known. No, their time should be structured. Consequently, instead of playing *games*, they would play and watch *sport*. Sport was a particularly strenuous form of play mimicking warfare that had evolved in English public schools. Football doesn't only mimic, of course, it is also the real thing: that's where its strength lies, that's the source of its extraordinary hold over the lives of modern men and women. The vocabulary used in the description of team sports, for example, and in particular football, is drawn almost exclusively from the domain of war: 'do battle', 'defeat', 'victory', 'annihilate', 'crush', 'rout', 'trounce', 'overpower', 'triumph', 'prevail', 'David and Goliath struggle'. (Tennis and golf commentators are less likely to resort to this sort of vocabulary.) Yet it is used not only metaphorically – that's the point: lives really are at stake here, as they were in the Roman games. This is not just theatre, it is the Colosseum.

So, almost two centuries ago, instead of simply playing with balls, or sticks and balls, the masses were encouraged to play team sports in their free time: football and cricket. For sport to appear on the planet you needed two things: a ball and England. (My four-volume 1887 Russian dictionary, for instance, doesn't even have an entry for '*sport*'.) The English masses rather liked the idea of aping the upper classes, while those already at the top were chuffed to see the masses occupied with activities based on conservative values. There were doubters, of course: by the middle of the twentieth century the Eton boy Aldous Huxley, as well as his student at Eton George Orwell, had declared sport to be 'bound up with hatred, jealousy, boastfulness, disregard of all rules and sadistic pleasure in witnessing violence: in other words it is war minus the shooting'. Orwell was wrong about disregarding the rules, but in the case of team sports pretty much on the money about everything else. What he failed to recognise, as so many of his persuasion do, is that fighting is fun. Anything gladiatorial gives humans pleasure that at times borders on ecstasy. (Not only humans, actually: even my dog loves a fracas – she'll hurtle from one end of the beach to the other to join in.) Sport provides a kind of collective ecstasy we find nowhere else – not at nationalist rallies, not even at rock concerts these days – and the uninhibited public expression of emotion. Inside a stadium you can watch everyone else being emotional with you.

In fact, as Terry Eagleton has pointed out, football in particular offers people an experience of emotional solidarity they find nowhere else in modern societies 'to the point of collective delirium'. This is a real service. Once upon a time religion provided many with an experience of solidarity combined with pageantry – and still does on occasion, but more rarely nowadays in the West, except on the religious fringes. Sporting events, by way of contrast, are highly carnivalised in the twenty-first century: revellers paint their bodies, wear outlandish costumes, chant, play music, dance in the streets and consume staggering amounts of food and drink.

While football itself may be tribal, one of its great strengths is that at another level it is socially inclusive. 'Most car mechanics and shop assistants,' as Professor Eagleton sensitively puts it, 'feel shut out by high culture,' but not by football. Football turns every Tom, Dick and Harry into an expert, repositories of detailed knowledge about things of no consequence at all – strangely sterile knowledge, but knowledge nonetheless. Football, too, like warfare, and more than any other sport, tells you who you are. Television is useful to the employers and the political class in much the same way as football and cricket, offering to fill in the vacant hours of those who feel excluded by high culture with spectacle rather than ideas, but television doesn't tell you who you are. On the other hand, like sport, it makes some people very rich.

Professional football players, like professional cricketers or tennis players, are businessmen, selling their skills to corporate business. Their pleasure in the game is not the pleasure of leisure, but pleasure in doing something skilled (and glamorous) extremely well in the public spotlight, often in return for vast material gain. It's work, not play. The most outstanding players can even become commodities for sale to the highest bidder in their own right. The businesses buying and selling them to each other are stupendously wealthy: in 2013 the value of Manchester United was estimated at almost 3.32 billion American dollars. Sport, Rupert Murdoch remarked, is his 'battering ram', enabling him to breach our defences and relieve us in one way or another, particularly through pay television, of our cash. And there's nothing wrong with that, unless you object to corporate capitalism in and of itself, just so long as we remember that it's not leisure, and it's not play. Quite understandably, even the state broadcaster in Australia devotes massive amounts of time – up to a third of its television news where I live – to replays of, commentary on and the promotion of professional sporting events, either as sport or as news. Professional sport is never just play. It's crowd control combined with big business. People love it.

In a word, when a prime minister such as John Howard or Bob Hawke enthuses about sport, whether it be cricket, football or yacht races (a certain kind of yacht race, mind, not just Australians from the suburbs scudding across the water in boats), they are, I suspect, whether they know it or not, betraying not only a love of male display, but also, above all, joy at the sight of the masses corralled, for the most part safely, and very profitably, into enjoying the spectacle of fighting to win.

Non-competitive play

Almost miraculously, given the grip sport has on the public's imagination (and purse), as well as on the media, on schools, on governments and on business, people in their millions keep right on playing with others and alone in a wide range of non-competitive ways for the sheer pleasure it gives them. When not working, they might bushwalk, cross-country ski and go kayaking, for example; they might take photographs, collect netsuke or first editions, write poetry or family histories and sing in choirs; they'll certainly go shopping, eat out with old friends (and make some new big-hearted ones), take in a movie or a concert, chat over coffee; some will jog, go motoring in the country, learn the tango, go line-dancing, take up life-drawing, dress up as knights or hobbits, visit foreign lands, spend afternoons in art galleries, quilt and embroider; and multitudes will worship (play at its most refined) and have flings (play at its best). While doing all these and a vast array of other things (beekeeping, for instance, or learning Esperanto, recording bird calls, skateboarding, dating online, knitting sweaters,

collecting vintage cars or Biggles books – the list is practically endless), we are not working, nor are we nesting
or grooming, we are at play.

However frivolous some of these pastimes may seem,
when we do these things we are at some level playing
at *re-presenting* an activity we feel in our heart of hearts
is fundamental to who we are, sometimes anciently. In
the case of religious rituals such as the re-enactment of
Jesus' last meal with his disciples or Shiva's marriage to
Parvati, we might hope to have an effect on a higher
order of reality. In re-presenting a more transcendent,
or at the very least overarching, order of things without
beginning or end, such as some deity's everlasting
love and mercy, we might even hope to influence the
operation of those realities in our lives: in silent prayer
affirming the deity's timeless, healing omnipresence, for
instance, or chanting a Durga mantra during Navratri
festivities in Udaipur. In the case of something like
stamp-collecting or shopping for a hat, this is less likely
to be at the forefront of our minds. All the same, if it's
play, and both collecting and shopping are, it's there.
Playful recreation really does re-create.

∽

What many people come up with when asked what kinds
of leisure they enjoy is a list of their hobbies. Shopping is

not a hobby, of course. It may be re-creating an ancient human activity, and in that sense be a form of play, but it's not, it seems to me – or is only for women like the Glenn Close character, living in Manhattan – a hobby. Why not? What is a hobby?

A hobby (*le hobby* in French, *das Hobby* in German and *khobbi* in Russian – the whole idea is as English as spotted dick) is a regular, to all intents and purposes non-competitive pastime indulged in purely for the pleasure it gives, not for material gain, just as watching television is, say, or pigeon-fancying or dawdling agreeably in department stores. However (and this is crucial), although no dictionary mentions the fact, I suspect that the word 'hobby' implies the gradual acquisition of skills, a drift towards connoisseurship, that exercising, watching television and shopping, even at Harrods, don't. Collecting, for example, is never mere hoarding, the art of bonsai never just a matter of keeping dwarfed trees in pots.

At the fluffier end of the spectrum, so to speak, the end where for the most part we're simply romping rather than performing to nourish the soul, the interest in connoisseurship is at a minimum. Collecting Coca-Cola bottles, for instance, playing bridge, owning a tortoise, doing sudoku every morning and meeting up with your friends for a drink and a chat every Friday after work may well be fun, demand some skill and absorb your attention regularly, but none of them can compete with playing the guitar, bird-watching or collecting Persian miniatures in terms of creating interconnecting webs of knowledge about the world.

All hobbies, though, at some level, deepen our experience of time. At the far end of the spectrum from collecting Coca-Cola bottles, there are hobbies that deepen our experience of time quite spectacularly: Freud's collection of scarabs, statuettes and rings from Rome, Greece, Egypt and, latterly, from China immeasurably complicated his notion of human civilisation as well as of the moment he was inhabiting. Even playing Broadway musicals on the piano every morning for ten minutes, or collecting carriage clocks, link us with the past in a way that amassing old Oxo boxes doesn't: there's social and musical history to acquaint ourselves with as we tinkle, and a wealth of information about clocks, travel, class and timekeeping across the centuries as we hunt down these exquisitely elegant timepieces.

Fecundity's the key. There's a scale of fruitfulness – or do I mean rooted creativity? – we can place our hobbies on. And on the fecundity scale there are few leisure occupations to match flirting with foreign tongues. I've been at it since I was about five years old, almost everybody I know has done it at least once, while some of my friends indulge in it on a regular basis: Italian, French, Bahasa Indonesia, Chinese, Esperanto . . . they dally with this one, then switch to that. Women seem especially susceptible to giving it a go. Yet it's hard to believe that learning Esperanto, however exhilarating and potentially useful it might be, and however many international Esperanto conferences in exotic locations you might manage to attend, could seriously compete with learning Indonesian in terms of fecundity or deeply rooted creativity – it was only invented by Dr Ludwig Lazarus Zamenhof at the end of the nineteenth century. (Not, of course, that it needs to compete. You can do both.)

What on earth do we imagine we're doing when we take up a foreign language for the pure pleasure of getting our tongue around it? On this fine Friday afternoon deep in the Australian bush, for example, by choice, apropos of nothing at all, I'm sitting inside reading an Algerian novel in French. At this precise moment I'm playing at being French. And I'm feeling very French indeed. *Très.* As I read, I take an occasional sip of my *grand crème* and have already eaten, I notice, two *galettes.*

If I look up at what's just outside the window, however, the game is over. I instantly become something more everyday, more quotidian; I go back to being someone who isn't remotely French. Out there it's all trees, utterly un-French trees – ridges and mountain-sides and blue-black valleys as far as the eye can see, thickly covered in trees (as well as leeches, snakes and wombats and God alone knows how many kinds of insect and bird). Between here and the horizon you can't see a single house or road – in fact, any sign that human beings exist. Even through binoculars it's just trees. Blue gums and white peppermints. Out the back of the house I grew up in it was also all trees – and leeches and snakes and God knows how many kinds of insect and bird, although there were no wombats.

For a moment or two, when I let my eyes drop back to my book, I'm not quite sure who I am: a Frenchman marooned in the Australian bush or a Sydney boy still dreaming he might miraculously turn out to be French after all. *À ce moment précis*, as we say (my mind is fizzing, it's a pot on the boil, it's a ragout of thoughts in several languages), I'm in Algeria – in Oran, actually (where I've never been). More particularly, I'm in a bar in Oran, the sort of place I would never in reality venture into late at night alone, and murmuring in my ear in French, French so sharp-edged it's cutting into my quick, French as faceted and lucid as polished crystal, is an Arab who does not exist. He's a character in a novel – two, actually, the one I'm reading and an earlier one by Albert Camus. (Which, by the way, is how Flann O'Brien says characters in novels should exist: in a literary limbo from which discerning authors can draw them as required, obviating tiresome explanations and precluding upstarts. Not that everyone agrees with him. 'That is all my bum,' says the narrator's friend Brinsley, being a character in only one novel.) What's going on? Who am I and what am I doing this afternoon? (And do you see what I mean by 'fecund'?)

The first time I can distinctly remember hearing a sentence spoken aloud in French I can't have been more than five. Over breakfast one morning my mother said, '*Passez-moi le beurre, s'il vous plaît.*' Why she chose the formal *vous*, I have no idea – I expect it rolls off the tongue more easily than the intimate mode of address – and whether or not she was then passed the butter I couldn't now say. In any case, it wasn't the butter she really wanted – even I knew that, however young I was – it was to make fun of my father's decision to add French to the list of tongues he had a smattering of. Although an essentially uneducated man, he'd been a seaman and so was well travelled, with a seafarer's Malay, more than a spot of Cantonese and bits and pieces of camel-driver's Pushtu from his childhood in Port Augusta at the end of the nineteenth century. Phrases and indeed whole sentences in these and other languages trailed after him like strings of memories of who he had once been. *Satu, dua, tiga, empat, lima* . . . I can still hear him counting the eggs after scouring all the nooks and crannies in the chookyard for them. And he had recently embarked on French. I do mean 'embarked', too: it was an escape from everyday life. He had quite a lot to escape from. My mother, feeling hopelessly trapped herself, had, I think, by that time given up on stabs at freedom.

At the sound of French I felt touched by a magic wand. I felt *turned into something* by the shower of sparkling syllables. I must have already heard quite a bit of it before my mother asked for the butter that morning because we had a cleaning lady from Noumea who came once a week and spoke French to me as she went about her chores, while the neighbour who kept an eye on me after school had a jovial French-speaking housemaid from *les Nouvelles-Hébrides* (wherever that was). All the same, '*Passez-moi le beurre, s'il vous plaît*' is the first complete sentence I have a clear memory of hearing and understanding. Like '*Je t'aime*' and '*Voulez-vous coucher avec moi ce soir*', it's not something you'd often have occasion to say in real life, but it's the sentence that launched me. I'm still flying – still learning, still talking, still reading, and still not quite French.

So what do I think I'm doing this afternoon, reading an Algerian novel and muttering to myself in French? It's quite an interesting novel, stylish, easy to read, but hardly (despite what it said in the *New York Review of Books*) compulsive reading. I'm not working my way through it because it's 'stylish' and 'quite interesting'. I'm refining my French, of course, but to what end? Unlike my father, I don't think I'm trying to 'escape' from anything . . . (I'm still thinking) . . . except, perhaps,

173

my ordinary life, *le train-train de ma vie quotidienne.*
(When you call your ordinary life ordinary in French, it
becomes instantly more interesting.)

My friend Suzy, on the other hand, who wouldn't
miss her Wednesday evening Italian class for anything
in the world, has no illusions at all about being Italian.
She's a Melbourne girl through and through, and all her
husbands have been either English or Australian. She
has no plans to read *The Divine Comedy* in the original.
She has vague thoughts of going to Italy at some point,
it's true – next year or the year after or possibly the
year after that – but then who doesn't? And who needs
Italian in Italy, anyway? The Italians couldn't give a hoot
whether or not you speak Italian, they just want you to
eat. Any Italian you might fancy meeting more mean-
ingfully is sure to speak some English, although his or
her mother might not. *Non importa* – just eat.

No, my friend Suzy, like at least half of my other
close friends, is learning Italian in order to lay claim to a
slice of cultural history she shares with the Italians while
disporting herself pleasurably in the company of like-
minded people. She has a passion for the Renaissance,
so it's the Italian strand of European civilisation she feels
herself most strongly at the end of.

Suzy has a small granddaughter – seven-ish, I would
guess, no older – who sometimes likes to try on different
clothes in the late afternoon – shawls, scarves, hats,

blouses – 'practising versions of herself', as Suzy puts it, walking up and down in front of the mirror. She's asking herself what she thinks of herself as a princess, a teacher, a nurse, a mother – and doesn't much want to be watched. 'And I'm doing much the same thing,' Suzy said to me, 'when I go to my Italian class: I'm asking myself what I think of myself as distantly Italian – as you and I are, after all, and almost everyone we know is, as it were.' I feel more directly French Enlightenment than Italian Renaissance myself, but I know what she means. This is leisure at its most lushly fertile. It's this sort of sense of things, surely, that the Catholic theologian Josef Pieper was gesturing towards when he wrote in his celebrated essay 'Leisure: The Basis of Culture' that 'leisure is possible only on the premise that man consents to his own true nature'. He and Suzy would disagree about what her 'own true nature' is, but the principle is the same.

Yes, at some deep level Suzy is honing a survival skill, but more immediately she's casting a spell on her daily life in one of Melbourne's inner suburbs, lending it an enchantment it would otherwise lack, whether or not she ever gets to Italy. She plays in a playground dedicated to teaching Italian for pleasure, plays with others at a specific time each week, and plays according to strict rules: Italians are tolerant of the rule-breakers, but all the same there are rules, and Suzy makes every effort to stay within them. Learning Italian is not relaxing, but then good play is often tense. Most importantly, however, learning Italian is a portal opening onto another world, one she has always felt connected to and endlessly interested in. She wouldn't get that with Estonian, say, or Korean, let alone Esperanto – or at least she doesn't imagine she would.

I've dallied with all sorts of languages over a lifetime for different reasons: Japanese for six months at university because I thought I should have a go at a language that wasn't Indo-European, and at the time Japan seemed to be the country of the future – but I was hopeless at it; nor did I have much flair for Indonesian, which I once learnt a little of as a politeness, expecting to visit Bali and Java, as we all did in those days; for much the same reason I learnt some Polish before setting out for Poland and some basic Finnish (a grammatically outlandish language) when I was living there in the seventies – quite unnecessarily, since any Finn I encountered spoke impeccable English; Greek took my fancy briefly when I was writing a novel set on Corfu, but I felt no natural affection for it; I toyed with Spanish, too, when I was contemplating a holiday in Spain once long ago, but there's no Spanish self hidden unhatched inside me; and German, of course, I learnt with considerable application at school, mastering it more as an accomplishment, like woodwork or touch-typing, than out of any affinity for it – it did save me from having to take chemistry, so *Gott sei Dank* for that at least. To be honest, I didn't become proficient at any of these languages, I was never tempted to don any of them like another self. At the beginning there was usually a moment, or a month or two, of spirited courtship, during which, like any swain, I mastered the superficial niceties – the accent, the use of the subjunctive and so on. But there was no genuine affair. I gave none of them my heart. French I did fall in love with, while Russian I actually married. (There are currently some tensions.) Once you marry a language, speaking it ceases to be a leisure activity, of course. You are no longer free.

Dallying with foreign languages is one of the few forms of leisure I am good at – less adept as I grow older, I must admit, but that's hardly a surprise. It's been one of the main ways I've tried to belong to a world in which it hasn't always been easy to find my place. Has it been a passion? It has certainly been one of my chief delights. I've been going to India quite often lately, yet haven't attempted Hindi or Bengali – I'm not sure why: after all, one of the attractions of the subcontinent is the sense that we belong to different branches of the same line of civilisation. On the other hand, I've always felt a yen to go further back and investigate Sanskrit – just for fun, just out of a love for language and history. In a word, for roots.

Night is falling here in the middle of nowhere. After dinner we have Claude Chabrol's *Les Cousins* to watch. It was made in the late fifties, if I'm not mistaken, so they'll speak clearly, more or less correctly, and never over the top of each other. Or else there's Fassbinder's *Ali: Fear Eats the Soul,* which I've seen before: it's about a German widow's affair with a Moroccan. No, today it has to be the Chabrol. Today I'm playing at being French *toute la journée. Ah,* it's six o'clock already and *le dîner est prêt!* 'Some bread?' *Oui, merci!* As it happens, it's from the French patisserie in Hobart – Jean-Pascal's. *Passe-moi le beurre, s'il te plaît. Merci!*

೧

We hardly need Freud to point out to us that most, if not all, hobbies also serve a deeply satisfying erotic side – paradoxically through failing to satisfy (as smoking does). Freud, as a collector of objects, was talking about collecting in particular, which he seems to have imagined was always at least unconsciously a fetish-istic activity, a replacement for something sexual we are denied or deny ourselves. I tend to think of most hobbies as faintly erotic for another reason: fulfilment is endlessly deferred. Gardening, for instance, which along with cooking can morph from nesting into a hobby, is never done; we never learn to play the piano well enough to entertain anyone but ourselves; caring for our pets is never finished; we play chess well, but we'll never be Bobby Fischer; collections of snuffboxes, postcards of Paris, Swatch watches or first-edition Enid Blyton books are never quite complete – indeed, completion would be experienced as a kind of death. Why this is tinged with the erotic is obvious: lovemaking, too, is never done.

Interestingly enough, hobbies also engage with death at every level. Who would have thought it? Playing the bagpipes, feeding the goldfish, tending the cacti by the back door – 'engage with death'? Really? You can see some sort of connection in the case of collecting gallstones or Elvis memorabilia, but Sunday painting, dinner with friends or collecting vintage cars?

I'm stretching a point, naturally – that's why we have points – but it's one worth considering: all play, even out-and-out romping, draws its vitality from precariously straddling the line between remembering and forgetting. That is why it is so life-enhancing: to play is to choose to remember certain roots, to re-enact, to relive, to keep alive certain things from the past and not others. We are refusing to forget everything and to live totally in the present. (Even dressage acknowledges roots.) Little wonder Sigmund Freud began collecting only when his father died. A passion for Afghan rugs, Lalique or matchboxes, a delight in reading every evening, writing poetry or breeding pugs – it doesn't much matter what we collect or play at, although some kinds of play are certainly more fertile than others – to stop playing would be to come to rest in the present moment, knowing nothing but what we can see, hear and smell. Living in the moment, after all, is about as close to dying as you can get. Of course, you don't want to remember *everything*, that way lies madness, but creative play turns moments into hours, months and centuries. Death hovers, naturally, as we run with our dogs, feed our hens, read our books, mount stamps in our albums from countries and empires that no longer even exist, but we grapple with it. We do what we do in remembrance of things past. Which reminds me: Swann's heart was said to be a showcase of his affairs, a kind of cabinet of love's curiosities. His *heart*. No more needs to be said.

ﾉ

It may well be true that recreation at its best nourishes something fundamental in us, but what about jogging? Does jogging re-create anything vital to who we are? Is jogging even strictly speaking a leisure activity? Wherever we go nowadays in any city on earth – well, not so much in the crowded metropolises of Asia and Africa, perhaps, not in the middle of Calcutta or Lagos because there's no room on the pavements there, and not so often in downtown Tunis, say, for reasons

I need hardly list, but everywhere else – you have to make way for people jogging. Every afternoon at the rate of about one a minute they pass the spot where we park to walk the dog. The thin, the fat, indeed the obese, the fit, the flabby, the practically lame, the bald, the ponytailed (and in particular ponytailed blondes), teenagers, grandfathers, tall and petite, they all come pounding past. They waddle, they sprint, they lope, they power up the pavement and, of course, they jog. You think you're safe to open the car door and let the dog scramble out, but all of a sudden, naked thighs flashing (he appears to be wearing underclothes), damp with sweat, he's upon you, swerving to avoid your car door as he barrels up the middle of the pavement, eyes fixed on the horizon, *whump, whump, whump, whump*, you don't exist, you're just a hazard on his path, *his* path . . . and now, what's this? As you swing the door fully open again to let the dog leap out, an almost totally naked woman appears from the other direction, *whump, whump, whump, whump*, ponytail swinging, swinging wildly, in what one American cultural commentator, Mark Greif, has described as a 'controlled frenzy', here she comes, straight down the middle of the pavement, *her* pavement, shared space she has appropriated to herself, heading for you and the dog but with eyes staring straight ahead, ears blocked with buds, you fail to exist again, you flatten yourself against the side of the car, she's *jogging*, you see, and you're not. It's a depressing sight, this presumptuous invasion of public space by half-naked men and women displaying their body anxiety. Baudrillard claimed it saddened him in the same way a glimpse of people dining alone did. No wonder half the world is anxious about its body, given the sorts of magazines we devour by the million every week and the kind of threatening pictures of rude health plastered all over the weekend supplements. That said, most of us don't act out our anxieties about our bodies in the street, stripped bare and forcing our fellow citizens to move aside as we pass. And if jogging is re-enacting anything, that's what it is: a deep-seated, often narcissistic unease about the body along with a fantasy about a simpler world where bodies were better exercised – at first hunting and gathering, and in more recent millennia farming. Peasants don't jog. Enthusiasts like to imagine they're improving their cardiovascular health while getting high on their endorphin rush: leisure with health benefits. In fact, a match or two of table tennis with friends, or for that matter a little light self-abuse, would have the same beneficial effect on the heart and mood, with less risk of degenerative joint disease. (Fascinatingly, the risk is highest amongst those wearing headphones as they jog because they are less aware of the punishment they're inflicting on the joints in their legs.)

One thing that must be said for exercising in a gym is that a gym is a dedicated space. It's sham labour just as jogging is, and no less narcissistic, taking place in a mirrored space that reminds Greif of 'a well-ordered masturbatorium', but if you don't want to watch or take part in this parody of working-class life, you don't have to. In a word, it's more polite. In Greece two thousand years ago, the sons of the nobility went to the gym to make themselves more sexually attractive (to men). Labourers had no need to go, and women did not appear in public with no clothes on. It would be naïve to think that a desire to become or to remain sexually attractive to *somebody* plays no part in the modern passion for going to the gym, although, to be fair, some gym enthusiasts, and some joggers as well, are also probably looking for a radical way to take time out from sedentary, or mentally taxing, workaday lives – a way to 'unplug', as some like to put it. But leisure should be about much more than unplugging. A leisure occupation might inadvertently serve all sorts of practical purposes, but to be leisure it must be chosen freely for the pleasure it gives.

∽

Take shopping, for example. In the recent movie *5 to 7*, one of those heartwarming romantic comedies America churns out, a Jewish mother played by Glenn Close tells her son that she and his new lover, a married French-woman who squeezes him in between five and seven several days a week, are 'going shopping' together. It's her way of reassuring her nervous son that she approves of his new liaison. They're not going to go shopping *for* anything, they're just going to go shopping – look at things, try things on, buy things they don't need (women of their class don't *need* anything) and bond. They're going to play at gathering – with style. They will act out being the kind of women they at root are. The son is much buoyed. (It ends badly.)

Now and then I choose to shop purely for the pleasure it gives me, too, although I'm a man and my rung on the social ladder is well below Glenn Close's or the Frenchwoman's. I don't mean that I prowl the streets with the intention of buying something specific such as socks, but that I shop in the delicious old-fashioned sense, the Glenn Close sense, now disappearing along with so many other forms of play. Leisure shopping works best in department stores, some arcades and, as any traveller to North Africa or the East knows, in souks and markets. It doesn't work at all well in city thoroughfares lined with shops: they're not for playing in, they're for purchasing things in. With the arrival of the department store in England and France in the middle of the nineteenth century, and in Germany a little later, gathering (always basically women's work) could be re-enacted with panache and almost indolent pleasure.

Fortnum & Mason in London, official grocer to the Queen, claims to have been operating as a department store since 1707, but the honour of being the first department store in the world – along the lines of Le Bon Marché in Paris, Macy's in New York, the Wertheim Department Store and Kaufhaus des Westens in Berlin as well as Selfridges in London – usually goes to Bainbridge's in Newcastle upon Tyne, which first opened as such in 1849. The BBC's pick for the first is Harding, Howell and Co's Grand Fashionable Magazine in Pall Mall in St James's, but it only had four departments. To this day, it's the English word 'shopping' (still *shopping* in Russian, *das Shopping* in German, *le shopping* in French, although you can say *faire les magasins* or 'do the shops') that best captures the essence of this leisure activity – indeed, in Russian it is the only real possibility if you mean visiting shops in commercial centres and shopping complexes in order to pass the time of day and perhaps pick up a few items of clothing, accessories and cosmetics while you're at it – but it's not the word you'd choose to describe shopping for chainsaws or fruit and vegetables. I never liked the words we were taught at school for 'shopping' in foreign languages: they all meant 'to go out in search of provisions'. 'Shopping' meant much more than that.

When I imagine shopping, I'm more likely to think of David Jones, the grand emporium of my own childhood, the multistorey 'temple of consumption' (to quote the cliché) where a shopper and her friend could easily spend half a day foraging. Not hunting, by the way – the shopper in the street may be the hunted, the shopkeeper being the hunter, but the shopper in a department store is primarily a gatherer. In fact, a department store is neither a 'temple of consumption' nor a 'cathedral of commerce' (to quote another common cliché): it is not a place of worship, however sumptuous, but a purely secular playground.

It has rules, naturally, as any playground does: there's a dress code, there are standards of behaviour to be observed. This, by the way, is why Christmas sales are not shopping and nobody one would know would be seen dead at one: sales are warfare, the so-called shoppers are the rabble on the rampage, with permission to loot and pillage for a day. Or are they less a marauding army than ecstatic dancers from the Middle Ages? They, too, after all, swarmed through the towns and villages on religious holidays in an outpouring of profane joy, drinking, eating, and overrunning the bastions of affluence. Do they indeed have as much in common with rock concert audiences as with raiding parties? Something is being unleashed, you feel, at a sale, something visceral, although not a desire for sex.

Once, I remember, when browsing for fun in Sydney's most genteel establishment, I eventually found myself on the final escalator, rising to the seventh floor, the floor where I'd sometimes had tea and scones with my mother half a century earlier while listening to a dapper pianist playing romantic favourites on a grand piano. Occasionally I had even watched a fashion show of sorts with her, high up there in the sky with views across Hyde Park. We weren't rich by any means, but we *were* nice. Now, as I stepped from the escalator, an employee moved forward with a hard little smile on her face and barred my way. 'I think,' she said, casting a cold eye down at my shoes and jeans, 'you might find what you're looking for on another floor. Try the second.'

'What am I looking for?' I asked, intrigued.

'Nothing you'll find here,' she said. 'This is the seventh floor.'

'I see,' I said, but didn't really see at all. I didn't know that this was the floor visited by women who had been telephoned at home about garments just in from Paris, London and New York that might be to their taste. All I knew was that there were standards and I hadn't met them. I took the down escalator back to floors where the codes for pleasure-seekers were more lax.

The shopper in a department store may acquire foodstuffs, items of clothing or even household appliances as she strolls around the store, but shopping in this old-fashioned sense is only tangentially about consumption, as the Japanese tea ceremony is only distantly about tea. It's primarily about leisured play: re-enacting for pleasure something once fundamental to our survival. The time spent in a department store (but not so much in a street lined with shops, and never in a supermarket) is time out from ordinary life. It's primal, it's restorative and it's communal, unlike other kinds of shopping, particularly online shopping, which actively disaggregate society, as it were, breaking it up into a host of small components: individual consumers.

Speaking of re-enacting for pleasure something once fundamental to our survival, can it be true, as one or two theorists of a Germanic persuasion have alleged, that irregular erotic relationships (relationships that fall 'outside the social norm', in Huizinga's formulation) are indeed 'the most perfect example of all play, exhibiting the essential features of play in the clearest form'? (Here I am quoting the Dutch anthropologist and psychologist Professor Frederik Jacobus Johannes Buytendijk.) And, if this is so, does it help explain why we keep embarking on them with such a sense of exultation and so foolishly?

At least subconsciously, it may well be the case that illicit love-play is the epitome of play. In languages across the globe, dalliances of this kind are often described as 'play' and those who are up for them as 'playmates' or 'players'. Play, after all, connotes a freedom of movement within certain boundaries – there's a bit of play to a loose wheel, we say (even in Japanese); we speak of there being some room to play, or a bit of time to play with, despite deadlines or restrictions. And so, intent on a dalliance (which need not, strictly speaking, involve physical lovemaking), we typically look for gaps and fissures (in a roomful of people, in a schedule, in a set of proprieties, in a marriage, in the beloved's carapace of emotions or just clothing) where we might play. Between five and seven, for example, in the case of the Frenchwoman and her lover in *5 to 7*. There's barely a novel or movie I can think of that does not turn on the notion of dalliance (courtship, adultery, betrayal) and its consequences. To our chagrin, in real life the object of our affections is likely all too often to want at some juncture to bring the relationship inside 'the social norm' – to move in with us, marry us, or at the very least meet up with us every Tuesday over lunch at Monterelli's. But that would be nesting, that would not be 'play'. This is precisely the point at which everything goes fatally awry in *Last Tango in Paris* and ends disastrously in *5 to 7*: when one of the players wants to stop playing on a certain day in a certain place, ditch the rules and turn the game into ordinary old coupledom (with names in *Last Tango in Paris*; with marriage in *5 to 7*). Marlon Brando had to be shot. Lurching from one marriage to the next is not dalliance, although easily confused with it. Play (let's remind ourselves) is an activity embarked upon within accepted limits in space and time (your place on Friday afternoons while your partner's doing Meals on Wheels) with no thought of material gain (payment or gifts), under no compulsion, purely for the feeling of joy it gives you both. And there will be rules (never ring me at home, say, or call me Ron), but not those of everyday life. There may be an element of winning and losing; there may be an acting-out of true love, romance, sexual slavery – any number of scenarios. During the performance, it's tense, absorbing, entertaining, rhythmic, age-old, ever-changing, educational, beset with ritual, and afterwards you have an overwhelming sense of relaxation quite unlike any other in the world. At its best, it's perfect. At its worst it's a fucking farce.

On the surface, as the two old friends meeting for a meal in a New York restaurant in *My Dinner with Andre* conclude, you have an affair because you're bored. In a nutshell, even if you have a partner you love beyond words, you are suddenly aware of a certain predictability in your life and the need for more twists to the plot before you lose your stamina; of a sense of confinement, with few opportunities for escape; and at the same time of there being nowhere you'd want to escape to – of a surrounding emptiness. In other words, as Peter Toohey remarked in his *Boredom*, it's exactly like Böcklin's famous painting of Odysseus, trapped on Calypso's island, staring out to sea towards home, after she's offered him immortality in return for staying on her island with her as her lover. What could be more boring than Calypso every night forever? And what could be more dispiriting than that view of infinite water everywhere you look? Never mind about dopamine depletion: Odysseus is bored because he needs plot, the hope of change, freedom to move, choices. Calypso wants to turn a dalliance into eternal matrimony. He needs erotic adventure. We all do.

Or should a trip up the Nile or a week at Noosa be enough to bring us back to life? Instead of an affair, should we be content with popping into the nearest Flight Centre and booking ourselves a quickie getaway trip to . . . well, wherever we can stop being ourselves for a week or two? How about Nepal? The Himalayas always take you out of yourself.

∽

As far as I'm concerned, travelling eclipses all other forms of leisure. Tourism, where we give our time away from home to a business and pay it to manage it for us (two nights here, a week there with breakfasts, Economy flights all booked in advance, excursions and museum entrance fees included), has its place, of course. It's often claimed that the business of tourism was invented by Thomas Cook. In fact, in England Cox and Kings were selling leisure travel as a package eighty years before Thomas Cook began organising outings, while a couple of millennia earlier leisure vacations were big business around the Mediterranean, but probably not packaged. *Salve, mi amice!* You want a Nile cruise? Not a problem. Lunch at a top-flight establishment? Try this one. The Greek islands? Follow me. But there's no evidence that anyone in the Roman Empire was making money out of organising the whole kit and caboodle.

Ideally, while I can see the uses of tourism, I like to travel in a more unconstrained fashion, without buying back time I've freely surrendered to others. If learning foreign languages, along with amorous dalliance, are particularly refined and enriching ways to play, deepening our humanity in a way tennis doesn't, virtuoso travelling takes us to an even deeper, more luxuriantly bountiful level (or can do), allowing us to frolic with our Spanish or Cantonese while exploring foreign parts. Travel can also embrace a fundamental human form of play many of us in these disenchanted times find it hard to enact except as theatre: ritual. And how nicely a trip, a jaunt, a weekend away or a journey far from home can frame a dalliance or three. That, at least, is how I feel about it.

Millions would disagree, including my partner, Peter. He sees little point in leaving home at all to taste leisure at its finest, and he's in good company. Horace, for example, wrote, 'They change their sky, not their mind, who rush across the sea.' (*Caelum non animum mutant qui trans mare currunt.*) That's a curmudgeonly view, I think. If it's change you're after, don't rush anywhere. When I close my green front door to head down the steps to the taxi, airport-bound, I make a point of not rushing, and try to stay moderately serene, or at least unruffled, in an animated sort of way, for the duration of my travels.

To leave home *well*, I might add, you must first appreciate what you're leaving, and come home again at the end of your peregrinations bearing gifts of some sort – if there's one thing Enid Blyton taught me, it's that you absolutely must be home again in time for tea (as it were). And just as leisure is richer if your working life is satisfying, so travel is more restorative if your idea of home is many-layered, if home, for all its limitations, is good.

Be that as it may, it's always worth asking ourselves why we do it, even if travelling is one of our favourite ways of spending time. What is it about leaving home we enjoy so much? And how do we choose where to go when we do? (The answer to this last question can be especially revealing.)

At the outset a word of warning: we should never travel to improve our minds. Any sort of excursion has the potential to improve the mind, but don't leave home for that reason. To improve your mind, read a book or take a course in something or other. Travel is reinvigorating, as all good leisure is: it pleasurably restores *in* us something fundamental to who we have been. (A Jungian might call it our anima. I'm not a Jungian – or only when it suits me, as it does here. No better words come to mind.) As you travel, you recrystallise in a new shape with a fresh transparency. Even when you're no longer young – no longer even middle-aged in my case – and a virtuoso performance as a traveller may demand of one more stamina than can be easily mustered (virtuosity being the true antidote to the banal, after all, not excitement); even then, if you undertake it in the right spirit, travel can be revivifying – indeed, at a certain age is there not more to restore? When you're young it's more a matter of updating yourself, surely, than renewal.

But what is it about travel that's restorative? I'm not talking about mere movement – I don't mean popping over to Adelaide to see your mother, or spending a week at a casino on the Gold Coast. I mean leaving behind your ordinary life to romp and play with different selves by different rules in places where your workaday life will be difficult to bring to mind. At home one is more or less oneself – well, it's only practical. But when you travel you can enact a multitude of selves. Here I'm a prince, there I'm an adventurer, in Paris I am stylish, in London I'm invisible, I'm a pilgrim on the Ganges, I'm a pagan in Rome, I am utterly alone, I sidle up to death, I am intensely, even passionately alive, I am a time-traveller everywhere, swooping about amongst the centuries, I am *well* again. (In some countries I'm even tall!) At home, although I am many things, I am none of *these* things, nor ever will be, it's too late. When I travel, I am – in a word – free (in a Western sort of way). It's like being twenty again, except that I know more. There are cultures in which people seek to escape from the self by merging with a greater entity – a *communitas*, as one sociologist calls it, avoiding the now moth-eaten English word 'community'. I am a Westerner, though – and happy to be one, by the way – so tend to look for escape from the self in multiplying the selves I perform or inhabit. Without unflinching vigilance I find 'community' edges too close for comfort to 'mob mind'.

I am also cheating time – of which I am not master at home, or not completely. At home, at some level I serve, I am under orders. In the end time will win, I know that, but meanwhile, when I'm far from home, and the hours are not measured out one after the other in a strand, but lie pooled here and there around me, both shallow and deep, I can cheat. When I'm away on my travels my time is not so easily commandeered by others, not so split up into separate compartments by everyday demands – that's the essence of it. In his essay on the brevity of life (and how no life is really brief or long, just well or badly spent), Seneca says that it's his aim to prise his time from the grasp of others, to take it back and make it his own, spending it doing pleasurable things of his own choosing – to turn work into civilised leisure, in other words, or into *otium* as he called it in Latin, a word with little meaning for most of us these days unless we subscribe to the sea kayakers' newsletter so named. Seneca didn't have to shop or iron his own togas: he had slaves. He could choose *otium* at home. One of the most effective ways for me to prise my time from the grasp of chores and the demands of others, however, is to leave home – to travel.

Above all, when I close my green front door and head down the steps to the taxi by the kerb, I'm performing a ritual. It took me years to realise that that's what I'm doing, but I can see it now. Historically, going right back to paleolithic times, if the cave paintings are to be believed, humans have had a huge variety of rituals to choose from: ecstatic communal dancing, bacchic revels, gladiatorial contests, feasting, the Hindus' Durga Puja festival (amongst countless others), the Christian Eucharist, the Haj and what Barbara Ehrenreich calls 'a variety of forms of cruelty to animals', with regular bear-baiting, cockfighting and the ritual slaughter of sheep enjoying a lasting popularity. Authoritarian institutions such as the medieval Church, and political parties on the extreme left and right in modern times have fought to keep public celebrations under their own control (Easter celebrations once upon a time, and military anniversaries in Russia and North Korea), but as any belief in transcendent realities, even a future workers' paradise, has faded across the globe, so has ritual celebration. You celebrate a ritual in order to re-enact a higher order and at the same time influence it to re-kaleidoscope itself to your benefit: the rain-dance, not to mention Holy Communion or burning the dead beside the Ganges, are good examples of the essential ritual. To call sacred ceremonies of re-enactment in remembrance of a deity 'play' is not to denigrate the ceremonies, by the way, but to elevate the concept of play. They are the quintessence of humanity's striving towards transcendence.

Nonetheless, wherever the idea of 'a higher order' goes little beyond throwing out the present government, it's difficult to whip up much enthusiasm for any kind of celebration. What, indeed, is left? Christmas dinner with the in-laws? A booze-up on Anzac Day? The Saturday night chook raffle at the local bowls club? (That's more a routine, I suppose, although in a world with no notion of transcendent realities the difference between a routine and a ritual can be hard to spot.) For most Australians, for instance, 'celebration' is more or less synonymous with drinking alcohol to let your hair down. 'Let's celebrate!' means little more than 'Let's have a drink!' Something has gone from our lives, some portal has been lost sight of – I suspect forever.

All rituals call for preparation. Years ago, in a book I wrote with travel in Northern Italy at its heart, I fantasised about leaving home with just one small bag, walking to the tram, taking the bus to the airport, choosing a flight from the departures board, and taking off into the blue – slowly, everything happens with ceremonial slowness – towards something I might now call transformation. (Not beauty, although where I find transformation is mostly beautiful – well, not Calcutta, I suppose, at least not in any obvious sense, nor Moscow in any sense at all, so not everywhere, but most places.) So there seems to be something about the progress from front door to magic carpet and then up into the sky that I have long found exciting.

I didn't mention it in the book, but before leaving home with one small bag you must ablute. I delight in every instant of this performance, this ceremonial act, this cleansing rite in which I wash away, step by step, the crustier accretions of the domestic self – not everything because it is a purification, a renewal, not an annihilation of the self. Next, I re-anoint myself for whatever awaits me along the way – and that will almost certainly include more bathing. It's striking how often bathing becomes important when we travel: rivers, lakes, waterfalls, the ocean, even hotel swimming pools as way stations in disguise, all of them more than mere water. And whoever stocks the airport duty-free shops is clearly on to this cycle of cleansing rituals: anointment is in the air at airports across the globe, unguents and fragrances on display everywhere you look. The sort of anointment I need is more psychological, but something fragrant in a tiny bottle before I step out the door still seems appropriate. Lastly, like a temple devotee, I don the appropriate raiments: ironed, colour-coordinated, chosen with taste. And now, virtually costumed, immaculate, I'm ready to start my progress. My front gate is hardly a Japanese torii, one of those marvellous vermilion H-shaped gateways you must pass through at the beginning of the *sandō* (the way to the shrine), but it will have to do. I prepare inwardly – is that a safe word? – to abandon reason for intuition, as worshippers must, and intellect for feeling.

The point is that you don't just lob into a shrine. What precisely, by the way, in these days of disenchantment, is a shrine? It's whatever makes you gasp with wonder, the place where you are ravished with a transfiguring astonishment – and you deserve to gasp with wonder at least once every time you leave home. It's wherever you find the Great Mystery, the *mysterium tremendum et fascinans*, as Horace might have put it, the unpolluted place. For example, for me, two or three years ago, it was (quite unexpectedly) the Rohtang Pass – in the far north of India, 13,000 feet up on an Indian branch of the old Silk Road. Halfway to heaven it was, prayer flags fluttering, eerily empty despite the pilgrims in the distance, gaily coloured, trekking towards a sacred lake (every puddle up there in the Rohtang Pass being sacred). I felt I was straddling a frontier: behind and below me was India, ahead of me Little Tibet, as they call it, mighty walls of snow and rock, an abyss at my feet full of wind and silence you can actually listen to . . . frightening, really; sublime, engulfing. Nothingness and infinite wakefulness all at once. Here at last, after weeks on the road, home finally fell away and I was renewed – reborn, a Shintoist might say, but I'll settle for renewed, not being a Shintoist, although I can see how one might toy with the idea of it.

Once a year, as I say, I need to travel like this. Once a year at least I like to leave home. Travelling around my bedroom as Xavier de Maistre famously did is not yet enough. It doesn't *have* to be anything grand – the 'shrine' (as it were) that I've left home to visit doesn't *have* to take my breath away. Nor am I expecting to encounter some divine presence, as Shintoists do. At the heart of a shrine, you see, I expect to find not a god, but a self stripped bare of home. There are rumours that even in ancient times, in temples on the Nile or at Eleusis, it was much the same: once you penetrated the core of the shrine, in the holy of holies, you found just emptiness and a mirror.

To be blunt, I suspect that the shrine for many travellers these days is the hotel they've booked a room in for six nights (breakfast included), not a place of ecstatic devotion: the hotel will be their Shangri-la, their sanctuary, their Eden and their Arcadia, their Paradise before the Fall – as, indeed, the establishment's name by the entrance will remind them. Here nature is pleasingly 'straightened' (to use a Japanese expression), angels bring them food and drink, they are free of toil, their room may well have water views, infinity is a swimming pool (of all things), the sheets are always fresh and sex (even if illicit) is never a sin. The hotel is a place given over to pleasure, it has strict rules, it's a joy to be in, it's where you romp and loaf and preen and possibly play until the end (check-out at eleven o'clock), when, just like the Famous Five, you go home. Nice, of course, but somehow not quite nice enough. Does this sort of hotel remind me, in a tarted-up, over-the-top sort of way, too much of the 'home' I'm trying to escape?

You can't both renew yourself and be your own master just *anywhere*.

You *should* be able to – Khartoum, Devonport, Scunthorpe: in theory none of them should be out of the question – but few of us can. So how do you choose where to head for?

Can I say at the outset, echoing none other than Samuel Johnson, that lots of places are worth seeing, but not *going* to see – the Eiffel Tower, for instance, in my book; and, to be honest, I'd have to say the Taj Mahal and Uruguay.

As far as I'm concerned, for a place to be worth going to, three things must dovetail: firstly, it will ideally be somewhere behind enemy lines because that puts you on your mettle – so Canada is out; going to Canada is just like staying home, but colder. Canada is nice. Canadians are nice. You don't want 'nice' when you travel. The god of travel, after all, is Hermes – god of boundaries and boundary crossings, of transition and transgression, constantly darting in and out of enemy territory. In a word, he's the god of changing places. I doubt Hermes could even spell 'Canada'.

Uganda, on the other hand, is definitely behind enemy lines, as is Cuba (so far as I'm concerned), but neither of them strongly tempts me as a destination because I doubt I'd find myself interesting there. It's not a judgement on Uganda or Cuba, but on the match. It's like a conversation, really, any conversation that leaves you feeling elated: you want to be part of it so long as it makes you feel larger, richer and more interesting than you've felt up to now, so long as it magnifies something you cherish, so long as it makes what could feel un-remarkable (about you or the universe) remarkable, as someone you love does. To be remarkable in itself – as the Taj Mahal is, or Machu Picchu, or Angkor Wat – is not enough. It must make everything that has been ordinary about you now feel extraordinary. That's the second criterion in choosing where to go.

And the third thing I look for when I travel well is hunger: where you go should leave you feeling slightly hungry, should sharpen your appetite for life, not quench it. This is what the Rohtang Pass did for me several years ago, you see. I was in alien territory, I was doing something extraordinary and it also left me hungering for Ladakh further up the road on the edge of the forbidden. (I went there the following year – I couldn't resist – and looked right into forbidden Chinese territory.)

If your soul is truly vast, any place on earth should be able to resonate with some part of it, however small, but, to be practical, I look to where those three things promise to dovetail. Paradise, in my experience, is not really what you want at all.

∽

To play is to be master of your time: Aristotle knew it, Cicero and Seneca declaimed it, and philosophers from China to Europe's furthest reaches have given voice to the insight. In a particular place, for a particular period, observing particular rules, you can freely choose how to spend your time for the pleasure it gives you. It has no aim beyond itself. This is why the ruling classes, together with the priesthood and military, have insisted over centuries that work is sacred: while everyone else slaves (including the rich), they remain free to play their (often deadly) games. What on earth is 'sacred' about the obligation to work? This is the sort of humbug it's high time we cocked a snook at.

And speaking of Europe's furthest reaches, it was the Scottish writer Alexander Trocchi who warned in 1962 that this maxim for keeping the masses in their place might one day work its way back up the social pile to enslave the masters. Hugh MacDiarmid called Trocchi 'cosmopolitan scum', and in a way he was, but he also turned out to be right. Just over five decades later, our masters, along with the rich, are chained to their desks for as many hours a week as the working classes are to their machines, if not more, often having more to lose by choosing idleness than peasants and labourers do. Something has gone very wrong with leisure. Each one of us has the opportunity now to try to put it right.

A final word

Leisure, thou goddess of a bygone age,
When hours were long and days sufficed to hold
Wide-eyed delights and pleasures uncontrolled
By shortening moments, when no gaunt presage
Of undone duties, modern heritage,
Haunted our happy minds; must thou withhold
Thy presence from this over-busy world . . .?

Amy Lowell (1874–1925), 'Leisure' (1912)

Without leisure, a civilised life is impossible. Without leisure, we are sunk in barbarism. A 'glimmer of civilisation', interestingly enough, is precisely what Monsieur Gustave believed that he and his staff at the Grand Budapest Hotel provided in their own 'modest, humble, insignificant . . . (sigh) . . . Oh, fuck it' way, not just a nice time lounging about. It was a touch of 'humanity' in the slaughterhouse the world had become. There may be no single right way to live a civilised life (*pace* the priests and pundits), but without leisure – without what Amy Lowell calls the 'quiet, teeming vigor' of chosen idleness, without deep-rooted nesting and fecund play – we're left with a life of servitude. That's not civilisation. Who wants that?

The twenty-nine-year-old rap musician Bow Wow certainly doesn't: it was reported recently that he has just retired, having worked hard selling millions of records since he was discovered by Snoop Dogg at thirteen. Tom Hodgkinson, editor of *The Idler*, believes that Bow Wow can now realise his 'dream of leisure' and has congratulated him for 'setting a good example' to the rest of us. It's not one the rest of us can follow, though, if we're to decently feed, clothe and house ourselves. Or, for that matter, might want to: half a century or more of leisure starting at thirty after sixteen years of frenetic toil won't strike everyone as an ideal balance. How many of us would even know what to do with all those years of free time? Will Bow Wow know? I doubt it.

For the vast mass of humanity at this point in history (except in Italy), work is unavoidable and leisure in ever shorter supply. We need to find better ways to balance them. Ever since the industrial revolution the idea that work is what most deeply fulfils us has become almost universal in Western countries: unfree labour not only gives us the means to own the things we want (or think we do), it gives us our very identity. At present, even in highly developed societies, the majority of us work ourselves ragged at repetitive tasks all day most days of the year until a late retirement, beating death to the post by a whisker, while the unemployed do nothing at all. And at the end of the working day or the end of our working lives, when some possibilities for being the masters of our own unmeasured time do open up, we're apt to dream of mere entertainment rather than of leisure in its myriad, fertile incarnations. Is there not some way, in this day and age, of evening out the hours we work and the hours in which to enjoy our idleness?

For a start, if increased means and increased leisure – Disraeli's 'two civilisers of man' – were shared more equally across society, with more people working fewer hours, it would be a gigantic step forward in the direction of a civilised life for everybody. Given the technological advances of the last couple of centuries, the end of out-and-out drudgery might really be nigh across the social spectrum. Or is that just cockeyed optimism? In the early twenty-first century, 150 years after Disraeli noticed the anomaly of an increase in means *without* an increase in leisure, we still doggedly barter leisure for even more abundant means . . . in order to acquire more possessions: bigger houses, bigger refrigerators, bigger everything, multiple cars, electronic devices, television sets and lifestyle statements – bigger toys, in other words. Can we not imagine a world where more or less everyone works three or four days a week at creative, physically agreeable jobs with long holidays, indulging in hundreds, even thousands, of hours of deliciously fructuous leisure every year, loafing, nesting and playing to their heart's content? It seems that no, we can't. It was beyond the range of our shrivelled imaginations when first broached by thinkers such as Bertrand Russell and John Maynard Keynes in the early 1930s, and still is. These days nobody at all has any confidence it will come true in his or her lifetime. All we've been able to come up with so far on both the left and the right is either total work for everyone or total work for some and unemployment for the rest.

However, what anyone can do – *anyone at all* – is to make an effort to find a better balance in their own individual lives between work and leisure, or, if you're feeling ruminative, between having and being. The idyll of total leisure, for example, may not be as desirable as it sounds. Bow Wow should beware. After Tom Ripley whacks Dickie Greenleaf on the head with that oar, for instance, he retires in his mid-twenties to spend the rest of his days taking his ease in the French countryside. It sounds blissful (for Tom, not Dickie), but it doesn't quite work. For all his seeming nonchalance, there's a cloud of unresolved guilt and sexual anxiety hanging over him as he gardens, paints and polishes his French. From time to time he hankers after narrative thrust, provided as a rule by small outbreaks of the criminality, including murder, which made a life of leisure possible in the first place. Bow Wow's leisure will be earned honestly, of course, but all the same, Tom Ripley's failure to achieve happiness unalloyed through boundless leisure sounds a warning. Trollope's infinitely leisured classes – the cast of high-born nincompoops inhabiting the pages of *The Way We Live Now*, for example, the countesses and dukes and knighted aristocrats leading lives of vapid uselessness in London and on their estates – while less openly murderous than upstarts like Ripley, are slaves to their greed every bit as much as their footmen and peasants are slaves to them. Playing whist, for example, was Lord Alfred Grendall's 'only accomplishment'

    . . . and almost the only occupation of his life. He began it daily at his club at three o'clock, and continued playing till two in the morning with an interval of a couple of hours for his dinner. This he did during ten months of the year, and during the other two he frequented some watering-place at which whist prevailed. He did not gamble, never playing for more than the club stakes and bets. He gave to the matter his whole mind . . .

Nobody else in the novel, set in the 1870s, seems to have led a life of any greater consequence: gambling, hunting, dressing for dinner and then dining are pretty much all the men's lives consist of, while, if anything, the women's have even less substance, entirely consumed as they are with mating and its rituals. *The Way We Live Now* is, of course, a satirical novel. Nonetheless Trollope has a valid point to make, surely, about the impoverishment, even total bankruptcy, resulting from leisure unrelieved by even the hint of toil: it actually leaves you less alive, even if better-dressed, than it does those slaving to make it possible for you.

Seneca was scathing about 'toilsome devotion' to any kind of task, not just about lives possessed by 'insatiable greed'. From his admittedly aristocratic standpoint, such unremitting toil was a squandering of life, turning living into mere time. In *The Brevity of Life* he even refused to count amongst the 'leisured' those men who have themselves carried about in a sedan chair, always punctual for their outings as if missing one would break some law or other, and being reminded every day when they must take their bath and recline to dine. The notion of a free man voluntarily choosing slavery filled him with disgust.

The recent documentary *Jiro Dreams of Sushi* shows two contemporary Japanese sushi masters doing precisely this. Billed as 'the world's greatest sushi chef' and declared a national treasure, eighty-five-year-old Jiro Ono has a tiny restaurant in a Tokyo subway station, the only sushi bar in existence with a three-star Michelin rating, where he works day in and day out making sushi with his elder son, Yoshikazu. From my point of view, the film presents an almost mesmerisingly dispiriting picture of a life lived as a slave – in Jiro Ono's case, to Japanese haute cuisine. His every waking moment is dedicated to achieving culinary perfection – he even dreams about making sushi when he's asleep. Each day resembles in virtually every detail the day before. Little wonder the director chose music by Philip Glass, another devotee of minimalist repetitive structures, for the soundtrack. Jiro's elder son says, 'I wish my father could make sushi forever. But eventually I'll have to take his place.' Jiro says of him, 'My son must do this for the rest of his life.' It's an elegantly made film, but there's something about this picture of lives spent in total servitude – unrelentingly repetitive servitude, lives yoked to making perfect sushi – that crushes the spirit. The fashion for wabi-sabi has passed Jiro Ono by.

At least he and his two sons are conscious of their own supreme connoisseurship. The ambience in their cramped sushi bar is refined, their clientele upper-crust. Intriguingly, giving over his entire life to repetitive tasks is connected to a deeply felt satisfaction that the next generation will also give over its entire life to repetitive tasks, presumably on the understanding that the following generation will give over its entire life to repetitive tasks . . . and so on, into infinity. It's a total-work scenario. It was much the same in Eastern Europe in my youth: you work until you drop so that your children might work until they drop in a little more comfort, and their children after them in even more comfort, and so on, into the bright future – a bright future of total work with bursts of organised leisure at a reasonable price. Which is what we are focused on now in the West, especially in the United States and Germany, across all social classes. This is serfdom with mod cons. Two thousand years ago Seneca declared everyone 'wasted for the sake of another'. It's much the same today – plus appliances.

Emancipation is possible, but must be gradual. We're pack animals, not ants or wombats, and virtually all of us have to find food and shelter before we lie about or play. Few of us are in a position to do a Lord Grendall, for instance, even if the idea of it appeals to us – in fact, today's Lord Grendalls are likely to work harder than their servants, aware that more is at risk for them than their servants if they don't; and few of us have Jiro Ono's all-consuming devotion to a single skill. Most of us must continue to gather and hunt for a good part of the time we're awake, and cherish the option of loafing, nesting, preening and romping for the rest. What is abundantly clear, however, is that, just as travel is best when you love being at home, so the idling, nesting, grooming and playing are most enjoyable, are at their most restorative, enriching and meaningful, when the work we do has deep, spreading and acknowledged roots in our culture – as Jiro Ono's indeed does, despite its repetitiveness, although few in the crowd hurrying past his door to the trains are likely to be able to say the same.

Nonetheless, in the search for rewarding ways to hunt and gather, there's one trap it's worth avoiding: the temptation to turn a passion into a job, a pleasure into an obligation. How easily a sea-change (or tree-change), meant to whisk us out of the urban rat-race into a setting where our love of nature can fill our days with tranquil delights, in fact turns into a life of hard labour and pared-back comforts – with no master, but hardly off the leash. How often we hear people newly appointed to some position in business or the arts tell us excitedly that their new job is perfect because they've always been 'passionate' about the theatre, the environment or designing women's evening wear. In the end it might have been wiser to keep the passion as a passion and the job as something you really love doing or feel strongly committed to. Otherwise you risk being swallowed whole by what should have been the means to an end. (For me, writing is not a job.)

Turning an amateur passion into a career is not the only temptation for someone juggling freedom and unfreedom. As Adorno warned us way back in 1969 in his remarkably readable, if sour, essay on free time, no sooner is our time 'free' than we're besieged with offers to make it entertainingly unfree – in return for money that we must labour longer to make. Camping, for example, which he believes was once indulged in as a protest against the tedium of bourgeois life in general and an escape from the family in particular, has in Adorno's view become 'harnessed and institutionalised by the camping industry', which has 'forced' people to buy caravans and equipment, thereby 'functionalising' people's need for freedom. Most campers probably feel they're getting value for money: they're getting added pleasure through their purchases of accoutrements; camping is now a lot more fun. 'Pleasure' and 'fun' are not concepts Adorno addresses in his essay – in fact, 'pleasure' only appears in the essay once, accompanied by 'merely', and the syllable 'fun' only occurs in the word 'function' and its derivatives. Be that as it may, you can see what Adorno meant. He was vaguely on to something.

Whether lounging about, pottering at home, whether attending to our appearance and wellbeing or playing with others, we are all too apt to take the easy way out and simply hand over our freedom to others to shape and systematise for us – for money. You have two weeks off? You give them to a tour company to sell you things in while moving you about the landscape. You have an evening when your time's your own? The casino's doors are wide open. Eternity with basically nothing to do for most of it? A church near you has got a plan at a price to suit every pocket. Yes, one can see what Adorno was getting at . . . But all the same, if we're alert, we can stay relatively free, surely, and simultaneously enhance our pleasure in what we choose to do. Who cares if somebody is making a profit on providing us with services we enjoy consuming? Adorno, obviously, found the idea intolerable, but who else does? The very thought of trundling around the country with an expensive caravan – or 'dormobile', as he calls it – attached to the back of the car makes me miserable, I have no inner snail, but tens of millions of my fellow human beings find it lifeenhancing, especially with the family in tow. In the same vein, I consider yoga as bastardised Hinduism, sold to wealthy Hollywood stars such as Greta Garbo and Gloria Swanson during World War II by the savvy daughter of a Russian aristocrat and a Swedish banker, and then purveyed on an industrial level to the comfortably-off across the globe as a physical fitness program combined, miraculously and in defiance of its Hindu roots, with the parodic performance of a spiritual sacrament. I see it as corrupt. Hundreds of millions of people, however, believe that buying this product has changed their lives for the better. If the purchase is freely chosen, and gives pleasure, who am I to object? Ardent devotees from Greenland to New Zealand can testify to yoga's power to bring tranquillity and new-found vigour back into their lives, particularly after a messy divorce. Who am I to wag my finger? Its roots may have been corrupted, but they *are* roots. Wellbeing is never the point of leisure – pleasure is – but if there are health benefits to our pleasures, why not grab them? In the end, the only thing any of us can say when faced with a pastime we find vapid is: surely there are more fertile, less vitiated ways to spend your free time?

At the heart of any well-balanced life, I strongly believe, lies a liberating concept of time. Ever since clocks were invented in around 1300, the commonsense way to picture time has been as a chain of moments, hours, days and therefore years, stretching out behind and ahead of us into the surrounding haze – not exactly into eternity anymore, let alone Eternity, because both of these sit awkwardly with clocks. We humans hop from link to link with diminishing agility and then die. Brian Cox and Stephen Hawking doubtless have more intricate ways to picture time, yet even they probably fall back on the chain model most mornings when they first wake up: a string of oblongs bursting with duties and appointments. It's a model that, like clocks themselves, is easy for our masters to exploit to their advantage, parcelling up our time as it does in handy units they can put to efficient use in their enterprises, leaving us small segments of blank time to fill in or sell on to other providers of goods and services as we wish. After all, in industrialised societies it's the only practical way to view things, surely. Could industry even exist without it? It might eventually have to, but for now it keeps everyone in his or her place.

Apropos of eternity, I was delighted to find that the Anglo-Russian novelist William Gerhardie, once declared a genius by Evelyn Waugh but now quite forgotten, was of the opinion that, in idleness, 'eternity runs at right angles across every point, every distinct and separate moment on the line of one-dimensional time, perpetuating every single selected moment into eternity'. There are echoes here of Seneca's view that the wise man makes his life long by combining all times, even the future, into one, making all ages serve him as if he were a god.

Another liberating way to view time, I find, is as splodges lying in clusters all around me. Instead of hopping obediently from link to link along a chain towards extinction, I pause in a puddle of it here and wallow in a pool of it there; some of the splodges are roundish (siestas are ideally roundish, for instance, as is tennis), some raggedy (gardening and shopping for new shoes), quite a few are rhomboid (hours spent at the office – well, you have to eat) and some splodges have branching trails of water (your holiday in Laos, learning Latin) wherever you look; some sparkle (*The Magic Flute* last night with a special friend), some are rippled (Scrabble on Wednesdays, especially if Gareth's in one of his moods), some (your mindfulness class, for instance, since you stubbornly insist on going to it) are mirror-smooth. You zigzag from one to the other. You're not going anywhere – at least, you're not *heading* anywhere. Behind becomes in front sometimes and vice versa, the left turns into the right. Now and again somebody who feels you owe them something (and perhaps you do) will try to lasso you and drag you back on track, make you point forwards like a grown-up and start counting – minutes, hours, cents, dollars. It's futile to resist, but do it all the same.

Time, to misquote Philip Larkin, is indeed for being happy in, splodge after leisurely splodge. It's for magnifying your humanity in, for enjoying the flourishing of who you are in – for achieving *eudaemonia* in, if I might end on an Aristotelian note. There's no other good reason for staying alive.